HOW WAS THE GAME?

A Fan's Journey
Around Baseball

Rich Dubroff

Diamond Publishing Company

Baltimore

DIAMOND PUBLISHING COMPANY
BALTIMORE, MARYLAND

COPYRIGHT © 1994   BY RICH DUBROFF

LIBRARY OF CONGRESS CATALOGING-IN-PUBLICATION DATA

796.357   94-094135
                                 CIP

ISBN: 0-9640426-06

For my parents,
Nathaniel and Isabel Dubroff,
and for Susan, who never fails
to ask me: "How Was the Game?"

Introduction:
Don't Let Baseball Die

It's getting colder now in this part of the country, and even thinking about baseball won't warm me up. It will be several months until the season begins, and because of the cold, it seems as if it has been months since the last season ended. It's only been a few weeks, but with the end of Daylight Time, it sure gets late early, as Yogi likes to say.

I'm watching football now, and so are the lords of baseball. They're talking of wildcard playoffs and interleague play to hype interest in the game. It's still a fine game, though it could use some tinkering. The past few seasons have been rife with scandal, office politics that made it on to the front page, racism, xenophobia and labor wars. You see, they were right, baseball is a microcosm of American society.

From the mid-seventies to just recently, it seems, baseball had experienced a new golden age. There were no Ruths, Gehrigs, DiMaggios, Mays, Mantles or Aarons, but the sport seemingly was more popular than ever. Huge television contracts were signed, the average players' salary soared to over a million dollars annually, you could go blind reading all the new baseball books published, and in a development that helped hasten the fall of the game, so-called rotisserie leagues were formed. (If you need an explanation of that bastardization of the sport, stick around, I'll try and spare you.)

It was inevitable that the game's popularity would wane, or its popularity would cease to increase. The New York teams both stopped being serious pennant contenders around then. There was another time when that happened, and a similar hue and cry was heard throughout the land. It was a generation ago, when I was a little boy, enthralled with the game. Here it is, a quarter century later, and I'm supposedly a grown up, still more enthralled with the game, even after I've spent some time as a sportswriter.

The game was decaying, they said in the late sixties, there

1

wasn't enough offense, it was too slow, football was the coming sport, more in tune with contemporary youth, and if baseball didn't watch it, basketball might be the sport of the seventies.

Having grown up in New York City, the world's media capital, then, and to a somewhat lesser degree now, I believed some of it. Football was the coming sport because Joe Namath and the Jets were contenders, and the Yankees and Mets were not. After eons of desultory teams, the Knicks were exciting fans with a team oriented brand of basketball, and pitching was dominating baseball.

In 1968, Denny McLain won 31 games, Don Drysdale set a record for consecutive scoreless innings, and Bob Gibson finished the season with an ERA barely over one run per nine innings, and America yawned. Lots of America was working or in school when the World Series was on, and there weren't yet playoffs, or League Championship Series. The lords of baseball expanded to 24 teams, split the leagues into two divisions and inaugurated playoffs. In order to spice up the game, they shrank the strike zone and lowered the pitchers mound. They worried a lot about football then, too.

It wasn't until 1971 that a World Series game was played in the evening to make the game more accessible to fans. Today, with some games starting well past 8:30 P.M. Eastern Time, many fall asleep in front of their set. Writers from Eastern newspapers who struggle to meet their deadlines lead the campaign for daytime World Series games. They might not be such a bad idea, but I remember missing a lot of memorable games because teachers insisted we actually pay attention to our schoolwork. Many have to work, too, and their bosses may not think they bringing a radio or television to work is such a good idea, either. The World Series is a great time to live in the west. Games begin before dinner time, and end before nine. Baseball seems pretty popular out there, doesn't it?

I've been a fortunate man. I've been to every ballpark where major league baseball is played now, and a few where it is no longer played, and this is the story of what it's like inside those parks, how people in different parts of North America react differently to the game.

The game will continue to enjoy great popularity, though it is in need of some alterations. (I'll make some recommendations at the book's conclusion.) Maybe we expect too much of it, just as we expect too much of our Presidents. It is just a game, and though the writers who cover it care about it passionately, for the most part, it shouldn't matter if in surveys, football, or basketball have larger numbers of young adults watching. It's a good game, has been for years, and will be forever, I hope.

It can be watched on many levels. It's not hard to understand, and I think, it's easy to enjoy. Some come to marvel at the artistry on the field, some come to soak in the sun, drink beer with their friends, listen to the music, or just watch the people. In this book, I'll tell you about all of those pursuits.

It's a different atmosphere in each park, even those that may seem alike to those who watch games for a living. While America may be the home of homogenized Holiday Inns, McDonald's and charmless airports, baseball is unique because no two parks are exactly the same, just as no two games are.

By trade, I'm a television producer, and because I travel a great deal in my job, I've been lucky. I've gotten to see lots of different games in lots of different places, and I'm going to tell you about it.

A few years ago, I had an extra ticket one evening for an Orioles game, and I sold it to a gentleman from San Diego, who was travelling around, visiting ballparks. He sat between my friend Mike Klein and me, and we three ballpark wanderers talked about our favorites. At one point, Klein said that he thought a good idea for a book would be to tell fans how baseball was different in different parks, and he said, I was the ideal man to do it.

I think Klein was on to something, and I think we should start our journey where that conversation took place.

3

Chapter 1:

It's Still Baltimore, Hon

I'm walking to the ballpark now. When I was a child growing up in New York, Yankee and Shea Stadiums were always far away places. Perhaps I was taken twice or three times a season, and never in the good seats. The box seats at $3.50 were beyond our means at the time.

When I got a little older and could go on my own, I went more often, as often as I could afford. That wasn't too often. Still, sometimes I managed to get to perhaps a dozen games in my best years.

I arrived in Baltimore in 1980, having accepting a job for the princely sum of $12,500 a year. I bought a new car, my first, a stripped Toyota Tercel, found a small apartment in an area that reminded me somewhat of New York, and proceeded to miss home terribly. It was January, baseball season was several months away, football season was over, and there wasn't a basketball team in town.

I ran every night, read The New York Times, and closely followed the moves of the Yankees and Mets. I couldn't wait until baseball season began. I lived several miles from Memorial Stadium, and on my corner, which was on a small hill, I could see the park, if the skies were clear.

When the weather improved, and the defending American League Champion Orioles began play, I paid my first visit to Memorial Stadium. A friend tipped me off that as the National Anthem neared its end, the fans would shout Oh!--say does that star spangled... I had always wondered, watching on television, why the fans did that.

I never had to pay for parking. He showed me a great area, just a few blocks away where I could park. A few years later, someone else showed me an even better area, which allowed me to be home twenty minutes or so after the final out.

On Monday evenings, all box seats in the upper deck sold for just $3, and if I decided to go at seven, I could get there in plenty of time for the first pitch. The $3 seats were fine, often right behind the plate, just above the press box. This was going to be all right. If I had only remembered to avoid the crab cakes in the early years.

Later, the crab cakes improved, and so did my finances. In 1982, several of us from work pooled our money and bought two season tickets in an outstanding location, thirteenth row, midway between home and first. In fact, our seats are slightly better at Camden Yards, and we now have four tickets.

The ballclubs in the early 80s were fun to watch. The pitching with Jim Palmer, Mike Flanagan, Scott McGregor and Steve Stone, among others, was consistently excellent. Eddie Murray was in his prime, Ken Singleton could still hit, and Earl Weaver, the fascinating manager, had a way with players who seemed on the surface, to be ordinary. Rich Dauer, John Lowenstein, Gary Roenicke and Benny Ayala were some of them. Weaver taught me more baseball than anyone, and he liked to say, "It's what you learn after you know it all that counts."

Early in Weaver's last year, a rookie third baseman was converted to shortstop. He was highly heralded, but no one dreamed he'd not miss a game for more than a decade.

Weaver tearfully retired at the end of the '82 season, and though I had only seen Orioles baseball for three years, I was hooked. By August of 1980, when the first place Yankees came to town for a crucial five game series, I had already switched allegiances.

It was Memorial Stadium that helped. From the outside, it was nothing special. It was round and concrete, and there was a sign on its front, "Time Will Not Dim The Glory of Their Deeds." I doubt that a dozen people who visited the stadium a season remembered what was on that plaque, but I never forgot it.

They named it for the men who died during World War II. There was an urn in the main lobby with some of their ashes on display. Nobody noticed. They were there to watch baseball, or football.

Names of stadiums are funny. So much energy is spent on figuring out a proper name. It took several years for the Governor of Maryland and the owner of the Orioles, Eli Jacobs, to compromise on a name for the new park. Governor William Donald Schaefer wanted "Camden Yards" after the railroad yards on which the stadium property was built. Jacobs wanted "Oriole Park" after the minor league ballpark where the old Orioles of the International League played. The original Oriole Park, less than a mile from Memorial Stadium, burned down in 1944. These guys finally compromised, a few days before the final game at Memorial Stadium was played. They decided on "Oriole Park at Camden Yards," which of course, no one calls it. The buses and light rail cars announce their destination as Camden Yards, but after a season there, Oriole Park doesn't sound half bad.

It's not like naming a child. The physical attractiveness of the park and its surroundings give the park its ambience, not a name. Who was Ebbets? He was the owner of the Brooklyn Dodgers early in the century. Wrigley Field was renamed after the chewing gum magnate who owned the Cubs. Shea was a lawyer who was instrumental in convincing the National League to return to New York after the Dodgers and Giants abandoned the city. By the way, Candlestick Park is built on Candlestick Point in San Francisco. Well, there's a location and name they wished they hadn't thought of.

Some called it Memorial Stadium. Others called it 33rd Street, built amidst a middle class residential neighborhood, several miles north of downtown, and about a mile east of Johns Hopkins University. Lots of people walked to the games, and there were literally dozens of access and egress routes. After a game, it was fascinating to watch each car or pedestrian head off in their own direction. In lots of stadiums built hard by highways, you'd sit in a line while hundreds of cars queue up to exit from those concrete jungles.

Here, there were white houses to look at over the outfield walls, and while the ballplayers didn't live in them now, they could have, and walked to play, not work.

When the Colts played and practiced there, some of those guys did live in the neighborhood. Flaky running back Alex Hawkins lived just a few blocks away, and was arrested in a local barber shop in the wee hours for participating in an illegal high stakes card game. When Colts coach Don Shula asked Hawkins about it, he told him, it was hard getting up a card game at that hour, and he wasn't going to be particular about his playmates. Besides, he always hated to wait to get his hair cut, he said. Time wouldn't dim the glory of his misdeeds.

Most of the Orioles who didn't reside year-round in the area lived in an apartment complex in Cockeysville, about a half hour north of the park. There aren't too many barber shops up there.

Most of the old ballpark's customers patronized barber shops, not stylists. Most of them drank National Premium or Budweiser instead of St. Pauli Girl or Corona, and a few of them, particularly those who drank a number of National Premiums, would find their way to the seats just in back of ours long about the sixth inning of three hour and thirty minute games. Some of them had tattoos. Some wore tanktops with obscene slogans. Others wore T-Shirts from "Hammerjacks," a loud and large nightclub hard by Camden Yards. These were not the type of the people one discussed the prospects for Perestrokia in the Soviet Union with. I became well acquainted with our local ushers. Many of these patrons found it difficult to get good seats at Camden Yards. They wrote semi-literate letters to the newspaper complaining that the team didn't understand their plight. They made semi-coherent phone calls to the sports talk shows. The Orioles forget who the real fans are. Those people from Washington are taking our seats. I didn't miss them much.

That was until I spent a season at Camden Yards. Camden Yards was everything Memorial Stadium was not. You would think after reading about it that Frank Lloyd Wright was the architect. You would think that Michaelangelo painted the outfield walls. You'd think that Abraham Lincoln had this place in mind when he scrawled

8

the Gettysburg Address on the back of an envelope.

It's a great ballpark, maybe even on a par with Wrigley Field, the major's best. But, come on, there weren't many real fans there. I guess real fans wear tatoos, drink lots of beer, and go to Hammerjacks. I'm not a real fan, then. But the preppies, yuppies and George Will look alikes that populated our section didn't belong there. George has his season tickets a few rows in front of us. He's not very friendly. Maybe if this baseball book sells as many copies as his did, I won't be friendly either. But, I won't wear bow ties to the ballpark.

When the nightly baseball quiz was flashed on the scoreboard, there were few people around that knew an answer. It wouldn't be a bad idea if there was a section in each park for the hard-core, non-beer swilling, non-cursing fan. There have to be more than four or five of us, don't there?

During the sixties and seventies, the Orioles had baseball's best record, and as their reward, they were supported miserably. It wasn't until 1979 that going to baseball games became the thing to do in Baltimore. That was around the time when Washingtonians began coming to the games, thanks to aggressive promotion on the part of the team. During the '79 season, the team was also purchased by a Washingtonian, the legendary barrister, Edward Bennett Williams.

Jerry Hoffberger, their long-time owner had decided that baseball's economics no longer made sense, and sold the team for about $12 million. Less than a decade later, after Williams' death, Hoffberger decided that the economics made more sense, and along with a group, attempted to buy the team, unsuccessfully for about six times his selling price.

Having arrived in town shortly after EBW bought the team, I was unaware of the enmity that Baltimoreans had for what they felt were snooty Washingtonians. I was well aware of the contempt that Washingtonians had for Baltimoreans. It was shared by much of the rest of the country. As Baltimore's reputation as the epitome of urban renaissance centers grew, the rest of the country tried to copy "Charm City's" model, but Washingtonians didn't.

Having lost two baseball teams within a decade due to lack of support, Washington was slow to adopt the Orioles as their own, but as the eighties progressed, it became increasingly obvious that D.C. would have a difficult time attracting a team. In their later years in Memorial Stadium, it was estimated that perhaps a quarter of Oriole fans were from the Washington metropolis, and judging from the cars in the parking lot across the street from the stadium, I found it hard to disagree.

Once Camden Yards opened, and seats were at a premium, those who rarely attended games before it became the thing to do, squawked that their tickets were being bought by these Washington people. Camden Yards was perhaps thirty minutes closer for these fans, and convenient to most Baltimoreans, except those who lived in the neighborhoods that bordered the stadium.

The team didn't begin to become extraordinarily popular until Washington fans adopted it. As any player will tell you, the larger the crowd, the better, and a season's attendance of two million, which wasn't achieved until the fan base got broader, was only a dream until the early eighties. Today, when Camden Yards' attendance easily eclipses three million, it's hard to remember that in the seventies, with quality teams, the Orioles had a difficult time drawing a third of what they draw today.

This larger fan base allows the Orioles to compete for free agents with larger market teams, should they choose to do so. It also allows the team to make record profits.

When the team raised ticket prices after their first season at Camden Yards, many were upset. In fact, it was a shrewd move. The team knew that demand for the best seats was immense, and that a club should raise ticket prices when the demand is highest. If they were losing regularly, and drawing poorly, it would be foolish to raise prices. (The team did lower prices for some seats which had inferior views.)

Since when did a fan have a constitutional right to attend a baseball game any time they wished? Though the state of Maryland built the stadium, the team belongs to its owners, and not the citizens of the state. It would be better if owners weren't able to force municipalities to build stadiums and arenas for their teams, but if Baltimore didn't build one, then someone else would have, and the team would leave.

Perhaps the press shares some of the blame for this culture of the fan that's grown up in America. If the fan pays their money, they have the right to boo, the old saw goes. That the owners of ballclubs have taken the fans for granted goes without saying, but just as a smart businessman is solictious of his customers, so should a smart baseball clubowner. If it's smart business to sell out your stadium in advance of the season, well, that's fine. Yes, that assumed arrogance may come back to haunt you in a few seasons, but let the market take care of it.

Do the people who call the radio shows actually go to the ballgames? If they had gone in as great numbers as they allege they had, the Orioles wouldn't have had to promote as aggressively in Washington as they did, and all the good seats would have gone to "Baltimore people," as they call themselves.

For some time, Wrigley Field and Fenway Park have been veritable sell outs from Memorial Day to Labor Day. People from surrounding states plan weekend or summer trips around going to the games, and while Camden Yards hasn't yet stood the test of time as Wrigley and Fenway have, it certainly wouldn't be surprising to see tickets remain at a premium throughtout the summers, at least, for the foreseeable future.

It is a lovely park. It affords a great view of the Baltimore skyline, and it's a relaxing view. Many new parks are built on parking lots, near highways, and have no great vista. Royals Stadium is a nice one, but it looks out on Interstate 70. If Oriole Park had been shifted slightly, it would look out on Interstate 95 instead of the Bromo Seltzer tower.

There are some many nice things about it. There's a great concourse that runs parallel to center and right field, where the everpopular "Boog's Barbacue" stands. Because the lines were so long, I've yet to sample one of former Oriole slugger Boog Powell's sandwiches. Besides, I was there for baseball.

The ugly warehouse that stands behind the concourse was the subject of much pre-season betting. Who would be the first player to break one of its windows? The smart money was on Sam Horn, the left handed power hitter, who was an occasional designated hitter for the Orioles. Horn hit just five home runs in 1992, none close to the warehouse. Shockingly to most, only three home runs even reached the concourse on Eutaw Street, and none came within twenty feet of the warehouse.

If a fan walked by the ballpark on Camden Street while a game was in progress, they could see part of the field. That was a great come on. With wrought iron gates and a brick facade, the park was welcoming. At first, I wasn't keen on the park's main color being green. In Yankee Stadium and the new Comiskey Park, blue dominates, and that has a nice feel, but as the season wore, the green grew on me. Since the park is sold out nightly, one saw huge patches of green only during the late innings of one-sided games, and contests that featured long rain delays. When a ballpark is always full, it sometimes seems ersatz. Those patches of green in boring games gave the park its final imprimatur, if you will.

I dreaded losing Memorial Stadium. It was so much a part of my adult life. Intellectually, I knew a new ballpark was needed, but as I sat in my seats, I would turn to my friends in the last couple of years there, and say, I can't believe they need a new one. I anticipated the final games there with a sense of dread. I thought I would cry when the ceremonies marking the final game concluded. I didn't, but lots of others did. By then, I had reconciled myself to the fact that a new ballpark was a necessity, and it would take some adjusting to, but it might be just as good, perhaps a little better.

I didn't visit the new stadium when it was under construction. Sure, I walked past there countless times, and sort of peeked in, but I wanted to be surprised. I didn't need to see my new baseball home under construction. I'd be there often enough, I rationalized.

As soon as the last game at Memorial Stadium was concluded, I began counting down to opening day of the new place, and the day before its official premiere, I decided that I'd pay a visit. The Orioles were working out on the field, and I sat in my seat, and then I took a look around. Not bad, I thought. I could walk there in half an hour, and take the new light rail home for night games.

The next day, when the first game took place, I was convinced. There wasn't a comparison between homey Memorial Stadium, and Camden Yards. The fans didn't call you "hon" much anymore, but the seats were close to the field, there was lots of leg and wiggle room, and the park was quirky.

I could have done without the tacky advertisements on the raised bullpens in the outfield, and though others liked the signs on the outfield wall, I thought, just because something was in older parks doesn't mean it was worth reincarnating. Even from my great seats, eight rows behind the Orioles dugout, just to the first base side of home plate, a ball in the right field corner can be obscured, especially when everyone in front insists on standing.

The park does have an old time feel to it, seats and roof like old Comiskey Park, center field bleachers like Fenway, but an ear-piecing modern sound system, featuring the absolute worst version of "Take Me Out to the Ball Game" imaginable.

I've been to every park in the big leagues, and I immediately ranked Camden Yards among the top in the game. I shuddered when I read of the plans for new parks in Cleveland, Texas and Denver. They would be based on the Camden Yards model. Please don't make these parks the nineties versions of Cincinnati, Pittsburgh, and Philadelphia. Allow them some local character.

It would be great if after a few years, when the novelty wears off, Camden Yards takes its place as one of baseball's treasures. It would be even better if I lived a full life, and Camden Yards was still standing and useful at its end.

Chapter 2:

Learning the Game in New York

At the time of my birth in 1956, there were still three big league teams in New York, three of the total of sixteen. A year later, two, the Giants and Dodgers, abandoned New York, and the attendance of the remaining team, the Yankees, declined. While the Dodgers found even greater prosperity in California, the Giants couldn't, and many New York baseball fans swore off the sport.

That is, until five years later, in 1962, when the Mets were born. This is about where I come in.

I began watching baseball a year later, attended my first game the day before I began grade two, at Yankee Stadium, and a lifelong passion, well, all right, obsession, was upon me.

I recall my parents deciding to take me to my first game, and this child of black and white television vividly recalls gasping at how green the grass seemed on the field at first sight. No one had color television, and photographs to a seven year old's eye, don't represent the sweeping majesty of that green grass.

The grass in neighboring Marine Park, or Prospect Park, wasn't that green, and artificial turf was still two seasons away. George Steinbrenner and the designated hitter arrived a decade later. (Isn't that a frightening thought? Steinbrenner and the D.H. arrive at the party together. No wonder you never see the two of them together in pictures.)

The South Bronx hadn't become the South Bronx yet, and the Yankees were still easily winning pennants, though the collapse, or in this case, for Yankee fans, the apocalypse, was only a number of months away.

I attempted to keep score at my first game. It was rudimentary, SO for strike out, GO for ground out, and I gave up after about six innings. I don't see too many seven year olds keeping score today. I don't see too many forty year olds doing so either. I always wondered why. It's a great way of keeping track of what's occurred, and if you keep scorebooks, you can quickly

14

recall games you attended, and check if you actually saw Cal Ripken's or Wade Boggs' initial games. (I did.)

I loved that first game so. I loved the green. Thirty years later, it still strikes me. When I was in college, about a dozen years after the first game, I looked up the box score of the game on microfilm to see how accurate my memory had been. I remembered that the Yankees had beaten the Detroit Tigers, 5-2. Al Downing was the winner, Frank Lary the loser, and that Roger Maris had hit a home run. Just to show you that my mind wasn't perfect at seven, I didn't recall that Joe Pepitone had also homered for the Yankees.

My parents took me to an occasional game growing up. They were casual fans at best, and even in the days before Bensonhurst, Howard Beach and Crown Heights, they were unwilling to allow an unsupervised youngster to take the subway to a game on his own. I was well into high school before I could take the ninety minute ride alone or with friends. Once, when I was thirteen, I stole away for an afternoon Knicks game at Madison Square Garden during Christmas holiday. The Garden was only about half as far as either Yankee or Shea Stadiums. I took the subway into Manhattan, and with several dollars in my pocket, this was 1969, walked up to the ticket window, and found, much to my displeasure that the matinee was a sellout. Fortunately, someone had an extra ticket, and I was able to gain admittance.

Naturally, during my afternoon absence, my parents needed to find me, and none of my usual pals knew where I had disappeared to. I forgot how I was able to explain my brief AWOL period, but I was frightened enough of my father not to tell him the truth. Besides, though he sort of liked baseball, he abhorred basketball, and I didn't want to get punished. Boy, that was a long time ago. Kids still worried about getting punished.

A few years later when I was just beginning Queens College, the Mets, who played at Shea Stadium, about a mile-and-one-half away, had qualified for the National League Championship Series. I had purchased a strip of tickets for their possible three afternoon playoff games. The first game of the three was on

Columbus Day. No classes, no problem. The third game on Wednesday, which loomed as the fifth and deciding game of the playoffs, was clear since I only had morning classes. The second game on Tuesday was a problem. I had a class or two, Political Science, or Sociology, or English, I don't remember. I'd just cut the class, I casually told my father. He non-casually slammed his fist on the dining room table, and informed me that I'd be attending said class(es). I did, and I don't recall cutting any classes during my college career. I also don't recall attending any other Mets games on weekday afternoons then.

These days, when I come to New York to work, which I do nearly every week, several times a season, I'll complete my work by mid-day, enough time to take the "7" train to the Willets Point-Shea Stadium stop and take in a game. My father doesn't object.

Though I didn't get my fill of baseball in person as a youngster, it created a hunger that has yet to be satisfied. As long as the weather is nice, and I have no pressing professional or personal responsibilities, I would attend a game every day if I could. When I'm off from work, I sometimes do.

New York was a great place to grow up. Though we didn't live "in the city" as Brooklynities referred to Manhattan, we thought of ourselves as just as sophisticated. In the sixties, and into the early seventies, there were still many working class people who lived in Manhattan. The West Side had lots of mom and pop stores, though we rarely went there. Brooklyn was our world.

We played all sports in Marine Park. Baseball, touch football, (I wasn't allowed to play tackle), basketball, sometimes roller hockey, soccer (there were goals in the park for the immigrant groups who played), and even an occasional do-it-yourself track meet was featured. We argued about politics, just as our parents did, and while we watched television, we read a great deal. All of our parents did, and they put a huge premium on education, and slamming fists on dinner tables, when attending postseason games was contemplated instead of education.

Most of all, we argued about sports. The Mets were new, and

they were terrible. The National League was much more popular in Brooklyn than was the American League. For some unfathomable reason, many kids would insist that you could be a Mets fan or a Yankee fan, but not both. With my profound nine year old logic, I would intone that since they never opposed each other in games that counted, why couldn't I root for both teams? When they met in a World Series, I could make a choice, I confidently reminded them. Nearly three decades later, I'm still waiting to make that choice.

There wasn't an ESPN then, or an all-sports radio station, much less a USA Today. Besides, my parents wouldn't have subscribed to cable if it was around then. (They don't today.) We had to satisfy ourselves with the glories of no less than seven New York newspapers, <u>The Times, The Herald Tribune, The Daily News, The Post, The Mirror, The World Telegram and Sun, and the Journal American.</u> My father purchased the Herald Tribune in the morning, and we took the Telegram, a Scripps-Howard paper, in the afternoons. Yes, people by the hundreds of thousands bought afternoon papers, then. I devoured the sports pages, though I didn't appreciate Red Smith in the Tribune, until I was nearly an adult. As the Mets floundered in their early years, the newspapers folded, and by the time I was ready for high school, just The Times, Daily News and Post were left. Newsday was just a Long Island paper that wasn't available in Brooklyn, and the Island was a million miles away as far as we were concerned.

I thought it was a gift from heaven, when on Saturday afternoons, I could watch simultaneously, the Mets on Channel 9, the Yankees on Channel 11, and the legendary Curt Gowdy on "The Game of the Week" on Channel 4. Little did I, or anyone else know, what would follow.

It was the center of the universe, New York was. It was the media capital of the world. We were the best and brightest because we lived there. We didn't know about New Yorker's arrogance. We didn't know, because as 11 year-olds, we were afflicted with it.

As the Mets and I grew up, we learned the game together. It was pitching and defense that led the Mets to their first World

Series in 1969. They played for one run, and often won by one run. The Yankees, meanwhile, often lost.

Though I read about other ballparks, Yankee and Shea Stadiums were my meccas, and they weren't bad places to learn about the game.

I've never read a travelogue about baseball parks which places Shea Stadium in the top pantheon of playpens. Of all the parks, there's little physical about it to inspire wonderment.

It's easy to reach via subway. Taking the elevated "7" train from Manhattan is a treat. It slowly lumbers its way through Queens and its ever-evolving ethnic neighborhoods. Irish and Italian a generation ago, now they're Colombian, Dominican, and Korean. If you're writing to an address in Queens, unlike the other four boroughs, you must direct it to a post office which tells you in what neighborhood your correspondent is located. On your way to Shea, you may rumble through Astoria, Sunnyside, Woodside and Corona before you land in Flushing.

If you're contemplating your first visit to Shea, sneak a peak at Manhattan as you enter Queens. The skyline looks as wonderful as ever, and if you look down, you'll see lots of subway cars, it's a repair yard. The train makes lots of stops, but within a half-hour, you'll see Shea on your left, the National Tennis Center on your right, and in the foreground, the Unisphere, symbol of the 1964 Worlds Fair. The Mets and the Fair arrived simultaneously.

It's fun riding the subway to Queens at the end of August and beginning of September when the U.S. Open is in session. People in tennis outfits riding the subway, and taking out second mortgages to purchase tennis gear displayed by the manufacturers. I've regularly attended the Open ever since it's been in Flushing, and always wondered why there was an article each year that mentioned how overpriced the food was. You'll never read an article that mentions how poor and overpriced the food is at most stadiums and arenas.

Several years ago, I discovered from a writer friend that there was no press room dispensing free and unlimited eats. Writers had to pay for the food with scrip, and wait in line with, and share tables with the great washed masses. It's easy to tell writers from the spectators. They're the ones not wearing tennis gear. In truth, the food is expensive at the Open, though there is quite a variety, and it is fairly tasteful. There isn't one ballpark where rotini and bagels and lox are available.

At Shea Stadium, pasta isn't available, but by the looks of the hot dogs, ptomaine poisoning is. I hold the record for most baseball games attended without consuming a hot dog; it always amazes me why supposedly intelligent people who never would eat a hot dog under normal circumstances feel it's unAmerican to attend their annual Mets game without eating one. People who like hot dogs tell me that the ones at Shea are among the worst they've ever eaten.

Why is it that in New York, home of many of the best restaurants in the world, has some of the worst ballpark food known to man? Casey's 37, located in the second deck, has passable roast beef and turkey sandwiches. For a long time, it listed betting odds on games, too. I guess baseball was so busy banning Pete Rose that they forgot to look inside their own ballparks to see that they were actually aiding and abetting gambling.

Shea isn't the best place to take your vegetarian wife. My junk food weakness is an occasional cheeseburger and french fries entree, and not only would Shea disappoint the non-meat eaters, you, my fellow meat-eater, would have to search high and low for one of the worst burgers known to man. They're not sold at many stands, and they're gray, small, limp, on a stale bun, and they don't put cheese on them. The fries are limp and tasteless, too. It's a good thing I don't go to the ballpark to eat. You might want to stop at a deli in Manhattan, and bring a couple of sandwiches for the train ride.

As for watching the game itself, it's far from the worst ballpark in the majors, I think. There's more foul territory between home plate and the backstop than anywhere, and the seats aren't close to the action. But, it's got beautiful natural grass, and it's outdoors. The scoreboard is extraordinarily large, full of useful information, including a permanant display of out-of-town games, which to my surprise, as I started travelling around baseball, was a relative rarity.

The sound system is loud and annoying. When a Met rally is stirring, a growling version of the beginning of Queen's "We Will Rock You" is played, hoping to stir rythmic applause. This is also heard in countless other sporting venues along with Gary Glitter's "Rock N'Roll, Part 2." You know, when the fans yell "Hey" after the music.

The skyline is industrial Queens, with an occasional flyover by a jet taking off or landing at nearby LaGuardia airport. It always seems gray out in the outfield. The park isn't enclosed, but no one stands on rooftops in the neighborhood to watch. That's because in this industrial area, there aren't any residents.

When the Mets were contending during the eighties, they sold out regularly, and this otherwise nondescript ballpark had lots of excitement. It's not a bad place to take an afternoon holiday on those occasions when the Mets play a weekday matinee. Schoolkids mix with brokers playing hooky, and it's a pleasant diversion.

If you can, try and sit in the loge, the second deck, right behind home plate. It was there in 1979, that on an afternoon in early April, I discovered the meaning of baseball life. Tug McGraw, long of the Mets, but pitching then for the Phillies, snapped off the meanest screwball I ever saw. How anyone could hit that pitch I'll never know.

Maybe you'll get lucky. If you're a baseball fan visiting New York, the odds are that the Yankees and Mets won't both be playing at home. It happens a couple of times a season, and perhaps the Mets will play at home during the day, and the Yankees will be home at night.

After the Met game ends, around 4:30 or 5:00, let's get back on the subway. You'll take the "7" train back to Manhattan, and at Grand Central station, you'll transfer for the "4" train, or at 5th Avenue, you'll switch to the "D" train. I prefer the "4" because the Yankee Stadium stop is outdoors. On the "D" train, though, you can marvel as it speeds non-stop from 59th Street at Columbus Circle to 125th Street. At one time, the stop before Yankee Stadium was 155th Street, the last stop in Manhattan. That was where the Polo Grounds, complete with bullpens in the field of play--in deep right center and left center fields, stood.

On the "4" train, you'll stop several times in the Bronx, and then at 161st Street, you'll first see it. It's blue and white, and more handsome by far than the neighborhood surrounding it.

The ticket scalpers will meet you when you climb down the stairs. In good times at Shea, they'll meet you on the platform, leading down from the train. Unlike Shea, there are actually businesses across the street from the Stadium, as it's known. There's a Wendy's, a couple of souvenir shops, a bar or two, and a bowling alley, with a McDonald's across the street. You might want to contemplate eating there because if you wait and eat inside Yankee Stadium, you may be stuck.

While the choices are much greater than at Shea, there's a food court down the third base line on the lower deck, don't expect prompt service. It's common for fans to wait two innings to be served, though the food doesn't look bad. The lines are shorter, and move quickly at the other stands throughout the park, but the ballpark staples of hot dogs, sodas, beers and pretzels are about the only foodstuff served. Perhaps the vendors at the food court ought to be paid by the customer rather than by the hour.

There aren't any ushers in the Bronx. Uniformed security guards, young toughs in police-like blue suits and caps patrol the stands, searching for miscreants. On one recent night, a fan briefly ran on the field, raised his arms in triumph, but alas, his victory was short lived. Two guards quickly caught him, dragged him along the field, and clumsily escorted him out through the third base dugout.

You may think you'll feel more secure with guards, but as a youngster, I relished the opportunity to beat the ushers. I was always on the lookout for a better seat. I'd buy a $1.50 general

21

admission ticket, which allowed you an unreserved seat in the third deck, which wasn't bad. But, I wanted to do better.

The trick was to act as if you belonged. I had a knack, and still do, of discerning, which seats are likely to be empty, and if you sat there, with your friends, and didn't create a ruckus, you were likely to be undisturbed. You'd bury your head in a scorebook, or just talk baseball. You wouldn't dare loudly cheer because that would call attention to yourself. If you were found out, you wouldn't want to trudge all the way from the box seats to the third deck, where you might get stuck behind a pillar. When Yankee Stadium was refurbished in the mid-seventies, the posts were removed, and so were the general admission seats.

Today, if you behave yourself, you can sit, it seems, in any empty seat. Without ushers, there's no one to check your ticket, and when I don't like my seat, I just move to a better one. The way the Yankees have played in recent years, there are lots of empty, better seats.

When the Yankees played exciting baseball in the seventies, with Thurman Munson, Reggie Jackson, Graig Nettles, Mickey Rivers, Willie Randolph, Chris Chambliss, Ron Guidry, Sparky Lyle and Rich Gossage, the crowds were rowdy. The pungent smell of marijuana filled the air. Once, at a World Series game, a fellow fan asked my friend, Boy Eugene, and I, if we had some rolling papers. Two non-indulgers we, we chose not to respond. After all, this was the World Series, and this jerk wanted to destroy his few remaining brain cells by smoking dope! We couldn't believe it. We stared at this moron in disbelief. "It's gonna be legal in ten years, anyway," he predicted. Yeah, and the Berlin Wall and the Soviet Union, would be no more, then, too, I silently thought.

Most times, the dope smokers brought their own rolling papers, and didn't foolishly rely on baseball nerds to supply them. It was a rare game then when that disgusting smell didn't permeate the air. I'm a lot older now, and I can't remember the last time I saw a joint at a ballpark, but if someone tried to do that today at Yankee Stadium, I'm sure corporal punishment would be meted out.

The old green Yankee Stadium facade that lined the upper deck no longer does. It's been painted white, and part of it hangs over the advertisements behind the bleachers. The monuments are still there. In the pre-refurbishment Yankee Stadium, a ball could be hit to center field, and get stuck behind the monuments for Babe Ruth, Lou Gehrig and Miller Huggins, though because it was so far from home plate (about 460 feet), it was unlikely. Today, they're not on the field of play, but in "Monument Park," which is open before the game, in the left field bleachers. Lots of plaques have been added to the original three monuments, including remembrances of the two Popes, Paul VI, and John Paul II, who celebrated masses there. The Yankees lead baseball in retired numbers, and many of those players are honored.

To me, the feature that best captures the majesty of Yankee Stadium is that voice. "Good afternoon, and welcome to Yankee Stadium," he intones. It's Bob Sheppard, with that regal voice. "You must not go on the field and interfere with play," he warns. "Let us now join with Robert Merrill as he sings our National Anthem." He expertly and delicately pronounces each player's name, taking special care to clearly enunciate each Latin performers name. You can be certain he'll not mispronounce Melido Pair-ez, as Per-ez, as most do. When Oscar Gamble wore an "0" on his back, it wasn't "number zero," as the uninformed public address announcers might call. It was simply, "the designated hitter, zero, Os-kar Gom-ble." He knew that zero wasn't a number.

On Mother's Day, you might shudder if Harry Caray sang "Let Me Call You Sweetheart," but it was perfectly all right if Bob Sheppard did.

These days, he spends some minutes before the game reading advertisements. It's not right. That voice shouldn't be selling stereos or lottery tickets, it should be calling, "in center field, number seven, Mick-ey Mon-tle."

He's been the public address announcer for more than forty years, and his voice exudes class, even if the rest of the Yankee organization doesn't. If you've never heard him, please go, before

23

it's too late, but remember, you must <u>not</u> go on the field or interfere with play in any manner.

Chapter 3:

The Keystone Combination

I never flew on an airplane until I graduated from college in 1977. I've flown on hundreds since then. I never saw baseball except in New York until the summer I was fifteen.

That year, my brother married a woman from Philadelphia, and some weeks later, they invited me to spend a night with them at her parents' house. I thought that would be fun because I discovered the Phillies were home that weekend. I talked my brother into driving me to Veterans Stadium, which it turned out, was about twenty-five minutes away, and in its first season.

Not long before, I was walking one evening on the handball courts in Marine Park, and I found, believe it or not, a neatly folded ten dollar bill. I saved it for a special occasion. My first game on artificial turf, now that was a special occasion.

In the late sixties and early seventies, old parks weren't celebrated as they are today. Forbes Field, Connie Mack Stadium, Crosley Field were relics, and it would be great, city fathers thought, if multi-purpose facilities could be built. Great for baseball and football, they thought. In truth, they weren't ideal for either sport. It wasn't until after the multi-purpose buildings became popular that it was decided that maybe it would be best if separate stadiums could be built for baseball and football. When Kansas City built Royals Stadium and the adjoining Arrowhead Stadium for the Chiefs, it was a sign that maybe somebody was listening.

Today, in Pittsburgh, Philadelphia and Cincinnati, there's talk of the baseball teams leaving the multi-purpose facilities by the end of the decade for new baseball only parks. The football teams can stay where they are, but those trend following owners realize they were wrong several decades ago.

Several decades ago, when I hadn't yet seen a game on artificial turf, I was astounded by what I thought was spanking new Veterans Stadium. Located in South Philadelphia, across the street from the Spectrum and JFK Stadium, then home of the Army-Navy game, it seemingly sparkled from its new stainless steel. It's actually concrete and round, but the image one takes away is of steel.

You entered about a third of the way up, and as you walked in you saw that each tier had different color seats. There were browns and reds and oranges and yellows, and the seats were made of plastic, not wood, and you didn't need an usher to wipe them off with a dirty mitten.

They had a scoreboard that actually had the image of the batter on it, and the turf was a darker green than I had ever seen before. If only I'd known the term radical back then, this was radical. But, I guess I did know the term, there was H. Rap Brown and Angela Davis, and Jerry Rubin. They were the radicals of the time.

I went home raving about the beauty of this place, and since I went more than a decade before I saw my second game there, I had plenty of time to reconsider my original evaluation.

As the old ballparks were razed, their champions grew more vocal, and the Veterans Stadiums of the world were figuratively trashed. Fenway, Wrigley and Tiger Stadiums were their ideal ballparks, baseball only, conveniently forgetting that football was played regularly in all three. The Patriots played for several years in Fenway, the Bears for many years in Wrigley, and the Lions for decades in Tiger.

Veterans Stadium is a drive of less than two hours from my home. It's also convenient by railroad; when you leave the train at 30th Street Station, home of Philadelphia's finest pigeons, take the green or blue line to City Hall, and transfer for the orange line. Take it to its final stop, Pattison Avenue, and you're at the Vet.

It's the closest place for me to get my dose of the National League, and though it has artificial turf, and it's enclosed, not affording spectators a view of South Jersey in the distance, it's really not so bad.

The fans are fairly knowledgeable and attentive. I say fairly because in 1990, perhaps a quarter departed on a perfect spring day after the Braves' John Smoltz had pitched his eighth inning of hitless ball against the Phils. If you were one of them, stop reading!

They're enthusiastic, too, and they laugh--especially at baseball's only worthwhile mascot, the Phillie Phanatic. He's huge, and green, and has lots of fur. He often sticks his tongue out, and he loves to dance. He's pretty good at it, too. Occasionally, he borders on the ribald, but I've spent many a game eagerly awaiting his appearance.

Before the game, he arrives from beneath the stands on his motorized three wheel bike, performing wheelies as the opposing players stretch and attempt to ignore him. Some do so at their own peril as he tries to attract their attention by edging closer and closer to him. If they're not careful, he'll abscond with their glove.

During the game, he roams the stands, and tries to amuse the younger fans, and the attractive women in the crowd. Between innings, he'll dance in the stands or on top of the dugout, often taking a lucky fan with him. Sometimes he'll try and annoy an opposing player or manager. A favorite target is Tom Lasorda. Once, the Phanatic took an overstuffed dummy dressed in a Dodger uniform with him, and attacked. Lasorda was enraged, and attempted to wrestle the dummy, who had the number "2" on his back, away. The Phanatic won that tussle, and now, when the mascot is on the field, Lasorda tries to ignore him, especially when the dummy with the number "2" is dressed in ballet tights.

Other mascots are easy to ignore, or just plain annoying. This guy is an actor first, and a mascot second. He's also been performing for fifteen years, and has only missed a handful of games.

For a multi-purpose stadium, it's semi-intimate. The seats in the lower level are fairly close to the field, though in a place that can hold 65,000, there are probably 25,000 that are

27

ridiculously far away. Baseball's lords seem to have been late at discovering the key to attendance. Keep stadiums fairly small, say 40-45,000. That way, fans will feel they have to get tickets early or else they'll be left with poor seats, or none at all. In larger stadiums, fans know they can always come to the park, and buy tickets. If the team isn't in contention, then attendance at these parks invariably lags later in the year.

There are lots of kids at the Vet, drawn by the Phanatic, lots of older people from the surrounding neighborhood, working class South Philly, and lots of young Rocky and Yo, Adrienne wanna-bes. You remember the Rocky movies, "southpaw, South Jersey, South Philly."

This being Philadelphia, you can buy funnel cakes and cheesesteaks at the concession stands. Funnel cakes are large mostly sugary pastries while the cheese steaks are thin slices of ground beef with cheese on a long roll, known as a hoagie. In New York, they're called heroes, in Boston, grinders, in New Orleans, po' boys, and most other places, subs. I have been known to have a cheesesteak at the Vet, though I'm not much of a funnel cake man.

In recent years, the Phillies have been disgustingly mediocre, so it's usually not difficult to buy some decent seats to go along with your cheesesteak. Without Mike Schmidt and Steve Carlton, the Phils haven't been contenders, but where else in baseball can you watch the Phanatic, eat a cheesesteak, and see Len Dykstra, too? They do have some characters in Philadelphia.

Once, after a late season game when Phillies outfielder Wes Chamberlain, standing on first base, jogged down to second on a 2-2 count and was easily tagged out, I asked Phillie manager Jim Fregosi if Chamberlain had missed a sign. Fregosi looked at me incredulously. "Was it a missed sign? What happened? He thought the count was three-and-two when it was two-and-two. It was a miscommunication between the scoreboard and Mr. Chamberlain, I guess."

The players, the managers, the fans, the mascot, they're all outspoken in Philadelphia. To the outsiders, the Vet may seem like just another antiseptic stadium, but I'm telling you, it's really not that bad.

At the other side of the state, rather the commonwealth, as Pennsylvania is known, is Pittsburgh, the site of another stadium that's really not that bad. This place is not that bad for different reasons, though. (I know, I know, the guy who's writing this is so hooked on baseball that he would say anyplace you watch baseball isn't that bad. Just stick around, I'll pan some places, I promise.)

Though Three Rivers Stadium is less than a five hour drive from my home, for some reason I had avoided it until 1989. One Sunday morning, I decided to drive there, and woke up early, and drove. It was located, I remember at the confluence. When Lindsey Nelson broadcast Met games, invariably once during a series, he would remind us that this stadium was located "at the confluence, where the Allegheny and Monongahela Rivers meet to form the mighty Ohio."

Walking the thirty minutes to the park from my downtown hotel, I passed pawn shops, hoary sandwich shops, some department stores, and I prepared to cross a rickety old bridge. Pittsburgh is full of bridges, many of which seem to be on the verge of falling, and as I espied Three Rivers, I thought, it was nice to be able to walk to the ballpark. I stayed at that Hyatt a few times, but on some subsuquent visits, I stayed at the Hilton, which was across the street from Point State park, and you could see the park from your window.

The walk was closer, across a modern, sturdy bridge, and if you looked left, you could see the Duquesne Incline. I've never taken the tram up, but I hear it's a great view of the area, and I promise to do it one of these trips.

Ferrys and steamboots toot away, and you can actually take a water taxi to the game. On a warm summer evening, it's a great walk, and you can if you're staying after an afternoon game, total your scorebook while sitting in the park opposite the stadium.

Before free agency destroyed the team, the Buccos, or the

Bucs, as they're known locally, were one of the best and most interesting of all teams. Bobby Bonilla, Barry Bonds, Doug Drabek, John Smiley, Jose Lind, they're all gone know, but the Pirates brilliant and self-effacing manager, Jim Leyland, remains.

Leyland hasn't managed in a World Series yet, but he won three divisional titles consecutively. He's one of baseball's best, able to judge talent, motivate them, and effectively communicate with both them and the media. Ask him why he changed pitchers on a 3-2 count, he'll patiently rattle off four reasons for the move. He's smart enough to know that he's the same manager who "lost 98---- games in 1986," as he'll often remind those who forget. Watching him work is a pleasure, and it broke my heart when the Braves scored three runs in the bottom of the ninth to win the 1992 National League pennant. I don't know how he stood it. He keeps vowing to quit smoking; you'll often see him sneaking a cigarette on the bench, and once he even used a nicotine patch, but boy, this guy is so wound up, he'll even make his guests nervous.

Inside the Bucs do what they can to make their park an inviting one. It's huge, seats about 59,000, though most of the playoff games in recent years haven't sold out, and it's lacking character. The fans aren't particularly informed, but the management is an astute one.

They cater to the cognoscenti, which most franchises ignore. Scoring decisions are announced quickly, and explained concisely. Difficult quizzes are given. (What team had gone the longest without being involved in a no-hitter?) The animated scoreboard displays were inoffensive. A laughing Pirate after the inevitable baseball bloopers, and the chugging and whistling Pirate express train, as the Bucs come to bat in their half of the first, so that the fans could be encouraged to lend their support to a nascent rally. If the Bucs trail heading into their last call in the bottom of the ninth, an ancient clip of the late John Belushi in "Animal House" yelling "Let's Do It" reverberates throughout the park.

Their attendance has been poor for such a fine team. Several reasons have been offered. The stadium isn't an attractive one, there aren't enough good seats, egress is difficult, the location, on the North Side of town carries a stigma, one Pittsburgher explained to me, and the ever-popular standard, the team has had too many black stars, and whites just can't identify with them. It's funny, isn't it, that in Portland, a city with a very small black population, that the Trail Blazers have sold out their games for two decades with an almost all black team.

The Pirates were the first baseball team to start an all-black team during the early seventies;the racial canard was heard then, too. Another old favorite, though not heard in Pittsburgh, is that the team doesn't draw because the neighborhood isn't safe. That was heard in the early seventies in New York when fans were supposedly afraid to venture to the South Bronx to watch the mediocre Yankees. It was also mouthed in Chicago when fans wouldn't venture to the South Side to watch the White Sox play in the old Comiskey Park. When the Yankees and White Sox began to win, it was amazing how safe the neighborhoods suddenly became.

I don't mean to belittle the fear of crime in urban areas. It does exist, though fortunately, I've not had a problem, at least attending sporting events. One venue that has had its share of problems is the Miami Arena, a breathtaking building, with a beautiful array of seats in various shades of purple. The white arena, in the outskirts of downtown Miami, is on the edge of the ghetto, and there have been a number of incidents, where fans were held up upon leaving. Professional golfer Jan Stephenson was assaulted there, and even at the Great Western Forum, Lakers General Manager Jerry West was robbed at gunpoint. A losing team scares people away much more than does the fear of violence.

It's also a fact of life that most of America remains white, and that they identify with white players. They seem to resent many blacks receiving what they perceive as outrageous sums of money, much more so than whites, in my opinion. White players are hyped, especially in basketball, where some teams in the NBA, haven't had any non-black players in recent years.

The success of Michael Jordan, artistically and financially,

31

is an exception to this theory. In fact, I, as a casual basketball fan, have become sickened by what I think is his overexposure. As a baseball partisan, I'm sorry that there's not a Jordan like figure in the sport, though I think the owners wouldn't know how to market him.

During the time I've been researching and writing this book, I've talked to a number of people in the game, and fans of it, about the absence of black spectators in baseball. Crowds at Washington Bullets games, which I occasionally attend, are perhaps a quarter or a third black, and football crowds have more black fans, though not nearly the number that basketball does.

When you've gone to a game, when was the last time you sat next to a black? Baseball has estimated that perhaps five percent of its crowd is black, though I would say it would be closer to two percent. I don't ever remember seeing a black fan in San Diego, Boston, Kansas City or Minneapolis, and even in Detroit, which is perhaps 75 percent black, the number of black fans is small. Fans there tell me that since Cecil Fielder's arrival, and his instant success, that the number of black fans has grown slightly.

In New York, Philadelphia and Baltimore, there are some black fans, probably ranging from between two and five percent. In Memorial Stadium, the surrounding neighborhoods were populated with many blacks, and it seems that more blacks attended games there than they do at Camden Yards. On my first visit to Toronto's Skydome, I was struck by the number of black fans I saw there, not a large number by any means, but more than you might expect in Canada.

There weren't very many black fans at all at Comiskey Park, in the South Side, but if you venture west a couple of miles, you'd be surprised that there weren't very many black fans at Chicago Stadium for Bulls games either--in an all-black neighborhood.

Perhaps the largest representation of black fans I found was in Atlanta, and as I recall, Oakland. Both parks are bordering black neighborhoods, and have featured many black stars. But, baseball has been slow to market to the minority community.

At the 1991 World Series, I got to talk to then commissioner Fay Vincent about that. He was sensitive to the fact that blacks don't attend many games. He said that he would hire a marketer, who was black, to attempt to increase black attendance. He did before he was ousted, and Vincent said that the food served, the music played, all had an impact, he felt on minority attendance. Latin Americans attended games, he said, in numbers greater than their population.

As long as I can remember, the Yankees and Mets broadcast their games on Spanish radio stations. The California teams do as well; the Dodgers and Padres seem to be particularly successful at drawing Mexican fans. The Padres go so far as to have some of their scoreboard announcements printed in Spanish. The Orioles began, during the 1992 season, to broadcast their games in Spanish.

Do the teams make similar efforts with the black community? Do they broadcast programs on baseball on radio stations popular with blacks? Do they take out advertisements in newspapers read by blacks? Many teams do sponsor little leagues in minority communities, and send players to speak to these youngsters, but if baseball wants to be successful in attracting black fans, and younger white fans, too, they're just going to have to be more aggressive. Basketball seems to have no problem marketing, and it's a shame that baseball, which I think is a far more intricate, and generally a superior entertainment product, has allowed itself to be beaten. (I'll have more specific thoughts in the books' concluding chapter.)

Until recently, it was necessary, to drive to and from Pittsburgh, to pass through a disgusting town, Breezewood. Located about 120 miles from Baltimore, a bit less than half way to Pittsburgh, it calls itself "the town of motels." Full of cheap motels, restaurants of various chains, and gas stations, Breezewood was a must see if you were exiting or entering the Pennsylvania Turnpike, on your way to or from route 70.

The city fathers had successfully lobbied so that there wasn't an exit directly from the Penn Turnpike to I-70. You would have to, often, crawl for even an hour or more, through Breezewood. Fear of Breezewood would keep me from making more trips to Pittsburgh. I don't like driving much even under optimum conditions, and Breezewood sent my blood pressure skyward.

Fortunately, there's now a way around it, though, it sometimes can add time to your trip. If you're on I-70, just continue on the new "National Freeway" until you reach Cumberland, Maryland, and take 220 north. It's a lovely drive, particularly in the fall, but it enables you to miss Breezewood, and hook up with the Pennsylvania Turnpike an exit later.

The food at Three Rivers isn't bad. Credible roast beef sandwiches and burgers are served, and for the younger fans, a "boardwalk" featuring all sorts of baseball skill tests is under the stands. It's always fun watching some apparently strong armed lad crank up his arm, and fling the ball at the target, and see that it measured at 53 miles per hour, about the speed of a Tim Wakefield knuckleball.

If the Pirates' fire sale renders them unable to compete in coming years, it will be a shame. Pittsburgh isn't a bad place, Three Rivers isn't all that bad, and I finally found a way around Breezewood.

Chapter 4:

Boston: The Most Overrated Place in America

As long as I've been an alleged adult, I've always heard how wonderful Boston was. What a great city, and what a great ballpark Fenway was. Well, they're half right. Fenway is great, Boston, I'm not so sure about.

I've been going to Boston since 1978, and while it's hardly my least favorite city, Detroit, Houston and Indianapolis have it beat by a lot, it's hardly my favorite. (San Francisco and New Orleans join it, I think, in the overrated category.) Almost every time I visit, the weather stinks. This, I can't understand. I've lived my entire life in the Northeast, and I think Boston should have the same weather patterns. Or, is it, that on my countless visits, the weather simply hasn't cooperated?

There's lots to see there, lots of good culture, the architecture is interesting, much history, and great hypocrisy. Boston is full of a bunch of quasi-intellectuals, who pollute the air with their quasi-intellectual theories on sports. (I'm going to exclude the Bruins from this argument because I'm not a hockey fan.)

These intellects think baseball is great, they write books about the Red Sox' supposed ineptitude, and the grave disappointments they've suffered through. The Celtics' tradition of outstanding play is great, too, and the celebrate the cerebral as well as physical gifts that their players possess. The Patriots are totally ignored. They play in Foxboro, about 25 miles from Boston, in the NFL's worst stadium, which is reachable by a narrow highway, and once there, fans park on gravel lots, and sit on benches.

I guess I'm just a little sick listening to these pompous self-appointed experts moan. 1992 was the Red Sox' worst season in a generation, but over the previous quarter century, granted they didn't win a championship, but they did win three more pennants than did the Indians, Cubs, White Sox and Astros, and they were regularly competitive, which is more than most of the afore-named franchises were. They just didn't "win the big one."

The Red Sox excellence should be cherished, instead of whined about. Over my years as a fan, they've had some truly marvelous players: Carl Yastrzemski, Jim Rice, Fred Lynn, Carlton Fisk, Wade Boggs and Roger Clemens. There were some great characters, too: Bill Lee, Luis Tiant and Steve Lyons. Name a few great Indians over that time. They just happened to lose two of the most celebrated games in baseball history, the sixth games of the 1975 and 1986 World Series. Yes, I would have pulled Bill Buckner out, too, and I wondered what John McNamara was thinking, then, but, lots of other teams would have loved to have been in a World Series. Sure, the object of the game is to win, but unless you've gotten to a Series, you can't win, and, since 1967, they've gotten to only one less Series than the Yankees have.

For many years, the Red Sox philosophy has been to play for the big inning. Over the last several, though, their power output has dropped. Some have blamed the construction of a new upper deck, which has changed the winds' direction. Others think their players just aren't as good. Over the last couple of years, the teams haven't been as interesting.

For nearly four years, the Red Sox were managed by a native of Massachusetts, Joe Morgan. An immensely likeable man, he was canny enough to cultivate the powerful Boston media. If you happened by his office, he'd ask you your opinion on how certain players were performing, and he acted as if he really cared. It was nice to have someone civil to talk to, especially someone who made up his own cliches as he went along. After a complete game victory by Roger Clemens over the Orioles in late 1991, Morgan was asked if he had any concern about Clemens' ability to finish. "You got the big horse out there, forget it, it's over," he growled, as he dismissively waved his hand.

Unfortunately, Morgan was fired shortly afterward, and replaced by the younger Butch Hobson, who was lauded for his communication and organization. These qualities led the 1992 Red

Sox to their first last place finish in 60 years, though injuries to Ellis Burks, Carlos Quintana and Mike Greenwell, didn't help.

For all the bellyaching about the Red Sox management refusal to recognize the importance of speed in a game, the fans turn out in great numbers. Sell-outs from Memorial Day to Labor Day are the rule, and they come from all over New England to watch. The majors' smallest park, seating some 34,000, it is a jewel.

Located just off Kenmore Square, it's great to see thousands of people walking to games. Subway and bus lines are minutes away, parking is dear, and so is the park. Intimate, with little foul ground, the fans are right on top of the action. The dugouts are located as far away from home plate, it seems, as any in baseball, close to the bases, and with the exception of a new press box on the roof, and some relatively new sky boxes, and a club where fans can watch the game and be served food, everything is the same as it was decades ago.

In 1978, when I paid my first visit, there was no upper deck. There still really isn't, except, for the modifications mentioned. The park is all green, the seats are red, and the food is pretty bad, with a limited selection. There are lots of places outside to eat, so don't worry. From the outside, it doesn't look like Fenway. I recall walking past the Green Monster on Landsdowne Street and finding it hard to believe that this was really it. If you take that walk, you'll see the enormous net that balls are hit into, and you'll see this park doesn't look much different from a warehouse from the outside. Inside though, it's still neat. Just don't listen to the fans. If you bring your field glasses, you can see the dents in the left field wall, and you can see, beneath the hand operated scoreboard, the morse code spelling of the late owner, Tom Yawkey's name.

The first time I visited was for a Yankee-Red Sox series in 1978. The Red Sox were far ahead, then, and the collapse was still more than two months away. I sat in the bleachers, the only time in my baseball life, I've done that, and tepidly cheered for the Yankees. They lost the two games I viewed, and Red Sox fans were confidently predicting a championship.

I almost drowned the first night. A sudden shower interrupted play, and as the large crowd in the bleachers attempted to make its way through the small exits, the rain fell harder. Since I couldn't move any faster, I felt helpless, and for a moment, thought I'd float away. (I can't swim very well.) Fortunately, I was able to make my way under cover, and after a brief interlude, the rains ceased, and play resumed.

In the mid-eighties, I arrived early to one game, and watched Dave Winfield enthrall the crowd as he tattooed the left field wall during batting practice as if he was throwing balls at it from fifty feet away. It reminded me of throwing a pink rubber Spalding ball against my garage or the handball courts at Marine Park. Do they still make what others called "Spaldeens?" I haven't seen one in years. The other kind were called "Pennsy Pinkies," and were manufactured in Pennsylvania, and as I recall, had a keystone insignia.

In 1991, I saw my first baseball game in a skybox, and it was at Fenway. In some parks, the luxury boxes are on the roof, an awful place to watch a baseball game. In some of the newer ones, they're about halfway up, but set back, a mediocre place to watch a game. In Fenway, they're on the top of the roof, on the same level where the old press box was, a great place to watch a game.

The box I was seated in was just off home plate, and allowed you an excellent perspective of the field. Foul balls came streaking back regularly, always a good test of the vantage point. The box had a refrigerator, full of beer and soft drinks, a table with hot dogs and potato chips, several easy chairs, a couch, a spotless bathroom, and a television set. The porch, which reached by opening the sliding doors had two rows of seats. Perhaps a dozen could watch the game from this box. On this day, just six people did, and I enjoyed it immensely. It was nice to be able to fetch chips and sodas when I wished, not having to wait in line for a messy bathroom, and Fenway's are among the messiest. Perhaps most important of all, it was wonderful to have ready access to replays on the television set.

Baseball is always looking for new sources of revenues, and I'll elaborate on how they can find some in the final chapter, but putting these skyboxes on top of an existing structure seems to be a fine idea. You don't displace any of your regular patrons, and it's an opportunity to add some corporate patrons you may not have attracted before.

From my perch, I could see the entire field, watch the pitching, and "get into" the game. Having luxury built into a ballpark constructed in 1912 seemed not in the least incongruous. It seems more ingenious.

With the Patriots seeking to leave their unsuitable facility, there has been talk that Boston would attempt to lure them back, with the promise of a new domed stadium. The idea of the Red Sox sharing such a facility would be the ultimate folly. Fenway Park must be preserved for as long as it is useful. Comiskey Park in Chicago had to go. Its facilities were poor, and it had little of Fenway's charm. Tiger Stadium ought to go, too, for reasons that will be discussed later, but with all the new stadiums in baseball, there should be a place for a ballpark that's small, the stuff of lore, and that's proven itself to be useful, and a popular draw.

Now, if you Bostonians would just cut out the unattractive carping, and appreciate what you have, then all would be forgiven. Besides, I kind of liked that skybox.

Chapter 5:

Chicago, My Kind of Baseball Town

Chicago is one of the most exciting of all American cities. It's
got a fascinating mix of ethnic groups, arresting architecture,
top-rate cultural attractions, wonderful restaurants, and a
populace that's manic about sports.

The Bears and Bulls have presented their fans with
championship teams in recent years, and tickets for their games
are hard to come by. The Black Hawks haven't won a championship in
a generation, but they're still mighty popular.

The last time a Chicago baseball team won a World Series was
in 1917, and though few fans alive recall that last White Sox
title, and fewer still recall the last Cub title nine years before
that, that doesn't stop Chicago fans by the millions from making
their way to two different and wonderful ballparks.

When it was new early in the century, it was dubbed "The
parlor park of the major leagues." When Ernie Banks toiled there,
it became "The Friendly Confines," and today, thanks to WGN, it's
in part a too trendy tourist trap.

Yes, it's Wrigley Field, and I never miss a chance to watch
a game there. It's changed in recent years as America has
discovered its beauty. Sit in the stands on a weekend, and you're
likely to sit next to someone who's attending their first game
there, but who is as familiar with the team as anyone who lives in
the Near North Side. In 1992, the Cubs became the first team in the
major leagues to vary their ticket prices based on day and time of
the game. Prices for weekends, holidays and night games, (there are
only 18 per year) are a dollar higher than they are for weekday
afternoon games. The crowd's different, then. During the week,
you'll still see many pensioners dutifully responding when public
address announcer Wayne Messmer reminds them to "have your pencils
and scorecards ready," so that they can jot down the lineups. The
older fans are harder to find on the weekends when the tourists and
kids arrive. One young fan kept annoying me during a visit when I

was trying to keep my scorecard. (I score each game in a scorebook that holds sheets for 25 games, and I save them, and often refer back to them.) This child wanted to know what I was doing, and as I tried to explain it simply, he told me he was from Kentucky, and visiting with his grandparents, and that he really couldn't abide baseball. He was about eleven, I guessed, and his foolish grandparents, who had spent $16 for his ticket, were only too happy to attempt to amuse this annoying child. They allowed him to buy many souvenirs of his visit to Wrigley, but I just wanted to watch the game. Next to me was a ballpark tourist from San Diego, who was touring the country in his quest to visit all of the major league parks, sound familiar? He was grateful to have someone to compare notes with, but his wife and children didn't seem too entertained by the action on the field.

Wrigley Field is, as they say, "a neighborhood ballpark." When the Tribune Company, the owners of the team, sought to play night games, the residents of the surrounding area put up a huge fight. They didn't want parking problems. Parking around Wrigley is extremely limited and costly (about $10). They didn't want drunks urinating in front of their homes at all hours of the night. But, they didn't want to be blamed for driving the Cubs to some suburban palace in Addison or Schamburg.

After several years of haggling, a compromise was reached. Night games would be limited to 18 a season, and they would begin no later than 7:05 P.M. In 1988, lights came to Wrigley, and the first game was promptly rained out after three innings were played.

Wrigley looks just as good at night. The lights are located on top of the grandstand, and there aren't any in the bleachers. The park is located several miles north of downtown Chicago, and you can get there by taking a bus, taxi or elevated train. The train rumbles through Chicago, letting you off just past the right field foul pole.

The neighborhood is a good one, well-kept with nice houses and apartment buildings, and lots of shops and restaurants. The park is surrounded by residences on Sheffield Avenue to right field, and Waveland Avenue to left. A cottage industry has sprung up in recent years by entrepreneurs eager to cash in on the popularity of the team. They sell "seats" to the games on the rooftops overlooking the park. Those fans, with their sunglasses and sun tan lotion feel as one with those in the park. They stand and sing along for the National Anthem, and during the seventh inning stretch, they accompany Harry Caray as he bellows: "Take Me Out to the Ball Game."

Watching a game there is great, but the creeping commercialism of the joint has gotten a bit out of hand. I fully understand the need for owners to maximize their revenues, and it doesn't bother me to see "The Friendly Confines Cafe" on Addison Street down the right field line, but hearing the starting line-ups or final totals announced brought to you by a sponsor is a bit much.

Fans are close to the field, perhaps closer than in any park in baseball, though Fenway and Tiger Stadium have some locations that rival Wrigley. You can actually feel the swing and a miss if you're sitting near home plate, and isn't it great to look at the hand operated inning by inning scoreboard in center field? It's a most relaxing place to spend an afternoon, and when the Cubs win, as they always do when I visit Wrigley, the flags with the current team standings in the National League are immediately replaced with a white flag with a large "W" for win. I hope they play ball there until kingdom come.

About six miles south, amidst the rubble of the South Side, it's new Comiskey Park. While the North Side features some of the tonier sections of the city, the South Side features some of the most squallid living conditions found in any urban area. Amid that squallor, when you take the train from downtown, it's somewhat amazing to see a circular stadium sticking up, seemingly from nowhere. From the train, it looks so out of place.

The White Sox played in Old Comiskey for eighty years, and several times over the years, the team threatened to move. Seattle, Denver and St. Petersburg were favorite destinations of the owners, though the St. Petersburg threat was taken seriously enough by the State of Illinois so that a new park to replace Comiskey was built across the street from the old one. In the final year of the old green park on 35th and Shields, it was exciting to see the new stadium come to life.

Many in Chicago were chagrined that the new park would have the same name as the old park. Charles Comiskey was the owner of the old Sox, and it was charged that his penurious ways encouraged his players to fix their World Series games against in Reds in 1919. For some years in the sixties and seventies, it was known as "White Sox Park," but when Bill Veeck regained control of the club in 1976, he ripped out the artificial turf infield and brought back "The Old Roman" in spirit.

The old green park with the yellow seats wasn't much to look at. The concourses were narrow, and seats were difficult to find with its byzantine numbering system. (Here's a thought: why can't ball parks have easy to discern seating? In Yankee Stadium, section 1 in the lower deck is behind home plate. The odd sections were on the first base line, and the even sections down the third base line. How can an outsider know that section 421 is a great seat, and that section 5 is a bad seat? Why not standardize sections so that section 1 is always behind home plate, and that even numbers go down the left field line, and odd numbers down the right field line? I know that seating in all ball parks is not the same, but it might be clearer to those who buy tickets from surly sellers at the box office, and it might discourage scalpers from attempting to convince fans that the two seats near the left field foul pole are just behind the dugout.)
The old park was one of the first to offer new and different concessions. The Mexican food was supposedly first-rate. I'm only an occasional Mexican food fan, so I never did try it, but the bathrooms were dank and hideous.

It was hard to hit a home run there, but its double decks and distant bullpens gave it a great old time feel. The organist there, the clever Nancy Faust, helped, too.

44

Fortunately, she's moved across the street to new Comiskey. The petite and perky Ms. Faust is now ensconced in a booth in the lower concourse behind home plate. Across the street, she was in the second deck, among her fans. She preferred it that way, but anyone who wants to talk to her can pop their head through one of the windows in the booth, or just walk in (it's unlocked.) I just walked in, and was treated to a virtuoso performance.

Faust is energetic, playing her complex organ-synthesizer with her right foot while her sneakerless left foot keeps time to the music. "It's more comfortable that way," she says. Her tunes are a mixture of contemporary pop, classic rook and ditties that were best forgotten. Her calling card for more than two decades has been the obscure rock song, "Na Na Hey Hey, Kiss Him Goodbye," by Steam, which she plays to mark White Sox home runs, victories and eaprtures by opposing pitchers. After several bars, the crowd begins to chant, "hey, hey, goodbye."

She's been playing for the White Sox for twenty-three years, through three sets of owners, and still excitedly looks forward to each game. "It takes me about two days to learn a song," and she doesn't use sheet music, but relies on her ears. In a day when loud recorded music has largely replaced organs around baseball, she's a delightful difference, bouncing her head in time to the music, and explaining how she decides what to play. If you want to talk to Nancy, it's best to chat when the opposing team is up, because she's busier when the Sox are up. When the Sox had players named Rudy and Vance Law, she'd greet their trips to the plate with "I Fought the Law, and the Law won," and when Kevin Hickey returned to his native Chicago to pitch against the Sox for the first time with the Orioles in 1989, she played "My Home Town," by Bruce Springsteen. She attempts to quell opposition rallies with "Stop in the Name of Love," and when a new team arrives in town, she carefully scans the rosters for interesting names and numbers. Wade Boogs must endure the Kentucky Fried Chicken theme, "We do chicken right," because he eats chicken before every game, and Tony Pena is welcomed by a vaguely familiar melody. "Do you know what that

45

is?" she asks. "That's the theme from the Motel 6 commercials, and he wears number 6." I doubt whether any of the 37,000 fans there could make the connection.

Faust, a native Chicagoian, was trained as a psychologist, but decided she liked playing the organ instead. Her mother encouraged her daughter with the good ear for music to apply for jobs at stadiums and arenas, and the White Sox hired her. For a time, she "played" for the Chicago Black Hawks, too, and she even moonlighted with the Minnesota North Stars. That ended when the owner of the Black Hawks, William Wirtz, decided that the popular Faust couldn't play for both teams, even though she had ostensibly obtained permission from the Hawks. "I just didn't get permission from the right person," she sighs. Now, she plays solely for the Sox, and at banquets and conventions, and during the game, often is asked for autographs. "Fans like to go home with something," she shyly offers when asked about her popularity.

She admits that even after nearly 2,000 games, she doesn't really understand the game. She gets involved with the action on the field, and thinks that "for the moment, I can do something appropriate, but when I get home, and someone asks me about the game, I can't remember anything."

Before she landed the Sox job, she had attended only one baseball game, and that was with her cousin, who worshiped the fine hitter of the late fifties and sixties, Rocky Colavito. I always liked the Rock, too, because we shared the same birthday, August 10, as does Nancy's cousin. I challenged her, and asked if I were a player, what would she play for me. For my name, she would have to play "If I Were a Rich Man," from Fiddler on the Roof, or if I wore number 10 for my birthday, she'd play "Ten," the theme from the movie, Bolero.

After "Take Me Out to the Ball Game," she plays something jaunty, and on occasion has even resurrected the song you may remember from grade school, "The Hokey Pokey." You remember, "you put your right foot in, you put your right foot out, you put your right foot in, and you shake it all about, you do the hokey pokey,

46

and you turn you yourself around, and that's what it's all about."
You probably haven't heard it in a couple of decades or so, but I
thought I'd remind you of it.

I did discover from Nancy the answer to a question that had
puzzled me all season. In many stadiums for both baseball and
football, and during basketball and even hockey games, I had heard
a familiar dirge played on the sound system. After a few notes, the
crowd would shout "Hey!" Everyone knew the tune, no one knew the
name. It was "Rock N'Roll, Part 2" by Gary Glitter. I felt relieved
as I learned the answer to my version of E=Mc2. Thank you Nancy
Faust.

When I walked inside of Comiskey for the first time, the royal
blue struck me. The stadium's primary color is that rich blue that
makes a ballpark look so regal. The concourses were
extraordinarily wide, and the locker rooms plush. The press box
was close to the action, too, just above the first deck, and a
visitor feels as if they're part of the game.

The upper deck seems miles away. In fact, I was told that the
highest seat in the upper deck at Old Comiskey was closer to the
action than the lowest seat in the upper deck at the new park. You
couldn't see the squallor from the stands, though. The park is
completely enclosed. It looks much like Yankee Stadium, both done
in blue, both located in neighborhoods in decline. Seats in Yankee
Stadium face the subway tracks and the wreckage of the South Bronx.
Fans in new Comiskey can drive in from the suburbs, and not have
to face the wreckage.

In mid-1991, when I made my first trip to see new Comiskey,
I was astounded to see part of the old park still standing. The
outfield stands were still erect, as was the old centerfield
scoreboard. Some of the old advertising was still visible, for the
Chicago Tribune, soon to be defunct Midway Airlines, and some
others, but amid the ruins, there was a new sign on the board, too:

"Speedway Wrecking, The Hardest Hitter of All."

47

Chapter 6:

On to the Regionals

You can find Cub fans in Portland, Met fans in Shreveport, and Brave fans in Anchorage, thanks to cable television. But, they're fans, not customers, as former Mets general manager Frank Cashen liked to point out. Customers actually pay their way into the ballpark instead of just watching on television.

It always bothered me that people could be Dallas Cowboys fans without being able to locate Texas on a map, and especially irksome was the "Subway Alumni," those Notre Dame fans who populated the bars of Brooklyn, cheering for the Fighting Irish. It was as if being a Notre Dame fan was a part of being Catholic in New York, even if you hadn't advanced past grammar school. There aren't any universities in New York that play major college football, so by default, Notre Dame became a quasi-New York team. Just ask some of these guys if they'd like to spend a weekend in Indiana, and they would have a seizure.

Part of baseball's charm is that, even before cable, people far from major league cities became devotees of teams. For decades, the St. Louis Cardinals were the westernmost franchise in major league baseball, and their radio network was the most extensive in the big leagues. Harry Caray's calls of the games were heard in California, simply because there was no team west of St. Louis. In 1955, the Athletics moved from Philadelphia to Kansas City, and three years later, the Dodgers and Giants moved to California, but the Cardinals still have one of the largest followings of fans around the country. President Clinton said as a boy in Arkansas he listened to Cardinal games. Today, the Cardinals, Cincinnati Reds and Kansas City Royals are special. They're baseball's regional franchises.

Fans from upstate New York come down to New York City to watch the Yankees and Mets, and yes, New Englanders consider the Red Sox their team, and plan their summer weekends around pilgrimages to Boston. But, the Cards, Reds and Royals are unique.

49

The Yankees, Mets and Red Sox play in large markets, and don't have to draw from miles around to thrive. These other guys depend on fans who drive in from as far as several hundred miles away to spend a weekend.

Just walk down the streets of Cincinnati on a summer Saturday or Sunday. It's a small big city, and it's all Red. Youngsters and their parents, too, are adorned in red. Hotels offer weekend baseball packages, and often it's hard to get a hotel room in Cincinnati for all the baseball fans from Kentucky or Tennessee or Indiana spending the weekend in the big city.

On the banks of the Ohio River is Riverfront Stadium. Steamboats toot, but the scenery isn't nearly as pretty as it is in Pittsburgh. The stadium is circular and made of steel, the same vintage as Pittsburgh and Philadelphia, and it has artificial turf, too, and a headache inducing organist, playing baseball's version of Muzak.

Downtown hotels are just a few minutes walk away, and as you make your way to the ballpark, licensed scalpers greet you. They're politely offering tickets, with large buttons featuring a Riverfront Stadium seating diagram. It's kind of fitting that in a city that continues to honor a convicted gambler, (Riverfront Stadium is located on Pete Rose Way) that ticket scalping is permitted. Just across the river is Covington, Kentucky, which reputedly was "a wide open town" several decades ago, featuring gambling and prostitution. Cincinnati also was noted for the Mapplethorpe case a few years back, when the local art museum was prohibited from showing some supposedly pornographic works. It shouldn't surprise you that this is the home of that doyenne of culture and literacy, Madame Marge Schott.

When I first visited Cincinnati, she was considered somewhere between a freak show and an annoyance. Whenever a local writer would make a scathing remark about her dog, she would have them banned from the press dining room.

One night, just before game time, Domino's Pizza made an unexpected delivery to the press box. Then Reds' outfielder Eric

50

Davis sent a pepperoni pizza to a banned writer, in the first case of a player ever buying anything for a scribe. The next year, pitcher Tim Belcher sent sandwiches to another member of the Schott list, who had accurately quoted his critical remarks about the pooch.

Schottzie, Marge's St. Bernard, died in 1991, and shortly thereafter, Schottzie 02 arrived. This pup cavorted on the field before games when players were attempting to exercise. She would nip at players and occasionally relieve herself on the field.

Marge feels Schottzie is an integral part of the Reds. In fact, when I visited the Reds' dugout, and saw a heavy bag just off the bench, I was convinced that the punching bag was lined with dog hair. Lou Piniella, former Reds' manager, was known not to be terribly fond of the pooch, and I know he would enjoy taking a verbal shot at her now and then. Baseball banned dogs on the field prior to the 1993 season.

Riverfront Stadium is probably the one most critics have in mind when they chide baseball for having "cookie cutter" ballparks. With its monotonous organ music, it's one of the least interesting ballparks in baseball.

It's perhaps the least expensive one, too. With the lowest ticket and concession charges in the game, Marge defended the charges of racism, in part by saying that she was struggling to keep the cost of attending games within the reach of the average family. In fact, a survey of all baseball franchises indicated that an outing at the Reds games was cheaper than at any other big league ballpark.

Fortunately, for 1993, the Reds brought back their uniforms of the sixties, with the pinstriped caps, and the red and white uniform blouses. A couple of years ago, at one of those "turn back the clock" days in Philadelphia, the Reds wore replicas of those uniforms, and they were far superior to the polyester models they wore for more than two decades.

I have a thing for uniforms, I have realized. My favorites are the classic Yankee pinstripe, so handsome and dignified, and the traditional Cardinal shirt. Those cardinals perched on a bat has been with us for decades, and I hope, won't ever change. I never liked the Pirates' seventies "mix and match" uniforms, where they have black, gold and white shirts and pants, and from day to day, a fan wouldn't know what they would wear. The Oakland A's of the early seventies vintage tried a variation on that, with the team wearing all white only on Sundays.

In my visits to the Hall of Fame, I would spend extra time at the cases bearing the uniforms of years gone by. The pre-World War I Philadelphia Athletics, with the stitched on elephant, all wool, looking as if they could afflict a wearer with heat prostration, was a fascinating one. Another was the garish red uniforms that the mid-seventies Cleveland Indians were saddled with. With their traditionally poor attendance, red was obviously the color of the ink on their books. Do you recall the Chicago White Sox of 1976 affecting the navy blue shorts and nineteenth century shirts? How about those of the San Diego Padres? Don't you remember those awful brown and yellows? On second thought, they're not much worse than the recent outfits of the Houston Astros. Tradition is best, such as the Gothic "D" of the Detroit Tigers, but I kind of enjoyed the road powder blues the Kansas City Royals wore in the seventies and for much of the eighties.

In case you haven't figured it out, I look for what other people may have missed. Once baseball season ends, I enjoy watching professional football, and I think I'm probably the only fan who can name all fifteen NFL referees, and discern the differences in their speech cadences. There's Jerry Markbreit, always eager to please the teacher. He was the little kid who sat in front of the class who reminded the teacher that they had yet to assign any homework. Gordon McCarter, always pompously explaining each call, and Red Cashion, yelling "Firrrst Down" on penalties that move the yard markers, as if he was a hog caller. For a long time, I thought NFL referees were all alike; they were all the same man, as airline pilots are. Can you tell one pilot from another? Can you tell one referee from another?

In the mid-seventies, when they miked the referees, it helped humanize and explain the game. It wouldn't hurt if baseball miked their umpires, and had them explain controversial calls. P.S. I also keep mental notes on each umpire, too.

Cincinnati's press box was a problem, too. It's enclosed, great for cold weather, but not so great for nice days, and although there are "no smoking" signs, several cigar smokers make for an unpleasant environment for the others.

In the front of the press box sits Old Joe. I never learned his last name, but each game, he collects a dollar from each writer in the attendance pool. Other favorite press box games are the no-hitter pool, and the total runs in a doubleheader contest. In the no-hitter pool, one draws lots on when the first hit in a game will occur. These contests were mighty popular in Cincinnati, along with Marge-bashing. Another game was to call Old Joe from a phone, and hang up. He'd scowl at the supposed offender, who would insist that they hadn't called. Perhaps some of the writers had their desks call Joe and hang up.

Joe was the biggest homer I've run across in a press box. After one game, he interviewed a Reds' player, since traded, and put his arm around him to assure him things would improve. It's no wonder that some of the Cincinnati reporters were so slow to catch on to Pete Rose's gambling, and so quick to defend him.

Cincinnati was the sight of one of my most embarrassing moments. When exiting the park on the way to the airport, I ran into several hundred of the Ohio Valley's best and brightest, the Reds youth. They were congregated by the player's exit, which I happened to use, and when they saw me carrying an athletic bag, they pounced. Perhaps I was the right age and size to be a ballplayer; more likely, they were desperate.

They began to plead for my attention. "Who are you?," they cried. "I'm not a ballplayer," I replied. That settled it. Anyone who claims not to be a ballplayer has to be one. You're just using that as a ruse so you won't have to sign autographs. Sign my glove, sign my ball, sign my program, mis-tah. Their shrieks grew shriller as I made my way to the stairway to catch a cab. I sheepishly tried to ignore the unwanted attention, but as I shook my head, they persisted. A couple shoved baseballs at me. Well, you little brats, if you're going to be so demanding, I'll just sign my everyday signature on your ball, I thought. You'll get what you deserve.

I signed my name, illegibly, because that's my everyday signature. It's also fairly large, but since they didn't know who I was, it would be their tough luck.

In other cities, kids would have books filled with baseball cards, and attempt to get their heroes to sign their cards. They would know whose autograph they were asking for. Here, when I began signing my name, the ear splitting pre-pubescent shrieking continued, and reached a crescendo. "Who is he?" "Who are you,?" they pleaded. After several autographs, one mom caught on. "What are you, a writer for <u>The Dayton Daily News</u>? She was one astute mom. If only her children could have been that astute, I thought, as I ceased signing, and trotted up the stairs toward my cab.

On just a few other occasions, I would be asked to sign my name, generally by an extremely small child, who thought any adult near a ballpark had to be a ballplayer. Once, in Arlington, Texas, I responded to a request by showing the child the standard admonition, "No Autographs," on my press pass. "That means I'm not allowed to give autographs," I explained. I conveniently avoided explaining that it meant that sportswriters weren't supposed to capitalize on their access to players to obtain their signatures, and then sell them to the highest bidder.

One of the richest franchises in baseball is the sport's original regional team, the St. Louis Cardinals. Owned for four decades by the owners of Anheuser-Busch, perhaps the Cardinals should have been tagged "America's Team" before the Atlanta Braves were by Turner Broadcasting.

The parking lots outside Busch Stadium are filled with cars from far and wide on the weekends. Illinois, Arkansas, Tennessee and Iowa license plates join those from all over the Show-me state.

Though Busch was built in the mid-sixties, when the other

multi-sport pleasure palaces were constructed, it's escaped a lot of the criticism that's been poured on Cincinnati and Pittsburgh. A fan can actually tell where they are from many parts of this park. Located just a short distance from the Mississippi River in downtown St. Louis, Busch Memorial Stadium was the first to be built in a city center in the hopes of helping to revitalize the town. While "Big Red," the erstwhile St. Louis football Cardinals played there, the place was built for baseball. Many of the visiting teams stay across the street at the Marriott, and the famous Gateway Arch looms behind the park. It can be seen from some seats.

The upper facade of the ballpark is arched, and happy, not monotonous organ music is heard. Naturally, Busch products are the only alcohol served, and the Budweiser theme song is played during seventh inning stretch in lieu of "Take Me Out to the Ballgame." That's played at the end of the seventh inning here. As the Bud song plays, the Anheuser eagle flaps its wings on the scoreboard in time to the music.

On my first trip here, during the 1985 World Series, the late August Busch, Jr. rode in an Anheuser wagon around the field, Clydesdales pulling, and as the Redbirds took the field, Ozzie Smith performed a backflip. He saves them for special occasions, such as World Series and opening day.

For an artificial turf field, it's surprisingly intimate. On my first visit, I sat in short right field, in a second deck box, and felt nearly on top of the players. But, I keep returning in my mind to the organ player.

A number of ballparks have organists. I've already expressed my admiration for Nancy Faust in Comiskey Park, and her talents, but most of them are forgettable. Pittsburgh's player is fairly clever, the woman in Los Angeles is stuck in a time warp, playing "The Mexican Hat Dance" and "I Enjoy Being A Girl." Atlanta's helped the Tomahawk Chop receive massive national publicity, and New York Yankees' long-time organmaster Eddie Layton does a nice job.

55

When I was growing up, I didn't know there wasn't a park without organ music, though on television, I could tell that at Memorial Stadium, they used recorded music. In the early days there, they had an organist, but they probably dropped it in a cost cutting move, knowing the Orioles.

Jane Jarvis was the Mets organist for nearly two decades, and her stuff was eminently forgettable, save for the Irish jig she played when Tug McGraw entered a game to pitch. Layton was much better;he began playing for the Yankees in the late sixties, and kept updating his inventory.

At the 1991 World Series, when the Metrodome organist began encouraging the crowd to rally behind the Twins with some sort of soporific chord arrangement, a writer from Canada began moaning, "sounds like hockey." I haven't been to a hockey game in more than twenty years, but I seem to recall that headache inducing pounding, attempting to rouse the fans. Let's ban rhythmic applause!

When I arrived in Baltimore, I had my first regular exposure to recorded music, and it wasn't bad. I'm not a music expert, or even a fan by any stretch of the imagination, but it was nice, between innings to hear something snappy. In Baltimore, they've tried with some success to be contemporary and original, although, some of their choices are a bit banal. They weren't the first team to choose "Wild Thing," as a theme song for their reliever, copying the 1990 baseball movie, "Major League." Nor were they the first to play the old Bill Haley recording, "See You Later, Alligator" when a starting pitcher left the game.

But, they were the first to play "Thank God, I'm a Country Boy" by John Denver at seventh inning stretch. That lasted a number of years, but today, that awful rendition, of "Take Me Out to the Ballgame," assaults the senses at ear-splitting levels.

Some teams, like the Phillies and the Yankees, use a combination of organ and recorded music, and I think that works best. A lot of younger fans, brought up on music videos, have no appreciation for the difficulty of playing an organ, and the subtlety, taste and knowledge required to do it well. Many older fans are uncomfortable with hip-hop and hard rock, and feel that an organ is nostalgic and unthreatening.

Even the Red Sox have changed. During the 1992 season, longtime organist John Kiley retired, and he was replaced by tapes. Kiley played a mean National Anthem on a most impressive organ, but his stuff was old! He made Dodger Stadium look contemporary with his "Seventy Six Trombones" and "The Beer Barrel Polka." At the conclusion of each game, win or lose, he played "and it's one, two, three strikes you're out, at the old ball game." The chronicler of "The Curse of the Bambino," the talented writer from The Boston Globe, Dan Shaugnessy, remarked, on the arrival at Fenway of contemporary music: "It's only Rock N' Roll, but we like it!"

At Kansas City's Royals Stadium, there's an organ, which on my visit there, bothered me. Whenever a Latin player would come to bat for the Royals, they played what passed, in mid-America, for an ersatz salsa ditty, in a vain attempt to stir the crowd. This was one of the few things that irked me about this lovely facility.

Though a non-midwesterner might think of Kansas City as being in the heartland, on my visits there, it's struck me as being closer in philosophy and topography to Denver than to St. Louis. At opposite ends of the state, about 250 miles apart, St. Louis and Kansas City are linked by Interstate 70, which passes just outside Busch Stadium. Drive about five hours, and you'll pass Royals Stadium, on the eastern outskirts of Kansas City.

When major league baseball was first played in Kansas City, it was played not far from downtown, in Municipal Stadium. How's that for an originality? In the sixties, in the American League, besides Municipal Stadium, there was Cleveland Municipal Stadium, Metropolitan Stadium in Bloomington, Minnesota, and Memorial Stadium in Baltimore. Was there any wonder that many said baseball lacked creativity?

Today, Arthur Bryant's rib restaurant, barbacued ribs, with the tangiest sauce imaginable, western fries and white bread to wipe your plate with, stands near where Municipal Stadium stood.

My visits to Bryant's are probably the only times I ate _real_ ribs. My stomach couldn't take Bryant's ribs regularly. The park wasn't far from the site of Wilbert Harrison's "Kansas City," either. You know, "Twelfth Street and Vine," looking for some "crazy little women, and I'm gonna get me some."

Kansas City is much more spread out than you would imagine for a relatively small big league city. The airport is at least thirty minutes north of the city, and not near anything. When it was built, those who planned it, thought that the area around the airport would be the next boom area. They were wrong. The Kansas suburbs, to the west, have experienced vibrant growth in recent years, and it's one of the longest rides from a ballpark or a downtown to an airport that I've experienced. Besides Shea Stadium, Philadelphia, San Francisco, Oakland, Baltimore and Atlanta are some of the closest franchises to airports, in case you're planning your own special "getaway days."

Royals Stadium is closer to Independence, Missouri, home of Harry S. Truman than to Arthur Bryant's. On my first visit to Kansas City, I hit Bryant's, the Truman Museum and Royals Stadium in one day, and it was a great day.

Royals Stadium, opened just months after Truman's death, is along with Arrowhead Stadium, the Harry S. Truman Memorial Sports Complex. In major league sports, I know of Robert F. Kennedy Memorial Stadium in Washington, the Hubert H. Humphrey Metrodome, and the Brendan Byrne Arena in the Meadowlands Complex in New Jersey. They're all named for Democrats. Even the lawyer William Shea was a New York Democrat. Why aren't there any sporting venues named after Republicans? Nothing after Eisenhower, Nixon, Ford, Reagan or Bush? The media must control the naming of sports stadiums and arenas, too. Annoy the media, demand that Republican politicians have some sporting memorials.

Christened in 1973, several years after the last in the wave of multi-sport stadia were foisted on this country, Royals Stadium was the first baseball-only park. Yankee Stadium, which has hosted a handful of football games since its remodeling, followed several years later.

Royals Stadium is the only baseball only park with artificial turf, a bow to the fans, who like in Cincinnati and St. Louis, come from hundreds of miles around to attend games there. Fans from Kansas, Nebraska and Oklahoma have adopted the Royals, and when they come at night, they see a spectacular dancing waterfall show in the outfield. They also a huge scoreboard, topped off by a Royal crown, and unfortunately, off in the distance, you can see, from many seats, I-70.

Besides artificial turf, the only thing wrong with this place is that it isn't downtown. Building ballparks and arenas near highways may be convenient, but it's cold. It's cold in the winter when the parking lot resembles a frozen tundra, and it's cold spiritually. You should see something besides parking lots and highways when you're leaving the park. Fans driving home should also be required to listen to the post-game show instead of Pearl Jam or the Red Hot Chili Peppers at deafening levels while drinking the beer they weren't allowed to consume over the last several innings.

When Royals Stadium was opened, it was hailed as a portent of things to come. Its seating capacity of about 40,000 was considered visionary, and two decades later, the Royals remain a healthy franchise, with creditable attendance, from a relatively small population base. Royals Stadium has stood up well, physically, too. With multi-sport stadia, the more seats the better. For football, Philadelphia Veterans Stadium seats about 66,000, and Riverfront and Three Rivers nearly that many. But, for baseball, today parks with about 40,000 seats are considered ideal. Camden Yards seats about 48,000, and the new parks in Cleveland, Texas and Denver will seat about what Royals' and Camden Yards do.

The three regional franchises each have hosted World Champion clubs within the last decade, making them artistically, as well as financially successful, as well. It would help ensure baseball's future if these regionals would continue to thrive. It would help if the people from either coast, who refer to these sorts of cities

59

as "fly over places" touched down occasionally. With their teams floundering, it might help them to see why baseball has such a hold on large sections of America--still.

Chapter 7:

The Golden State for Baseball

"All the leaves are brown, and the skies are gray," the Mamas and Papas sang in the sixties. "I'd be safe and warm if I was in L.A., California Dreaming on such a winter's day."

During the dead of winter, what they used to call the hot stove league, is when I think of baseball in California the most often. Southern California is one of the few places in the U.S. where you could play baseball all year round. The season is long enough, but on weekend evenings, after the football playoff games, and brisk winter walks, I start thinking of baseball. It's not quite halfway between the last out of the World Series and Opening Day yet, but it's getting close.

When I was born in Brooklyn, another brisk walk away from Ebbets Field, the Dodgers still called it home. When I was a year old, they played their final game there, and I grew up hearing my elders curse Walter O'Malley until they day he passed away in 1979. The Brooklyn Dodgers were the most profitable franchise in the major leagues, but playing in tiny Ebbets Field with little parking in the area, they were getting antsy.

Ebbets Field was located near several subway and bus lines, and a short distance from the lovely Brooklyn Botanic Gardens and Prospect Park. Many said it was in the "Flatbush" section of Brooklyn, but growing there, I found out that nearly half of Brooklyn could be labeled "Flatbush." It was near Flatbush Avenue, to be sure, but Flatbush Avenue stretched about ten miles, from the Manhattan Bridge, all the way to the Marine Parkway Bridge, which led to Queens. Ebbets Field was on the southern edge of what many Americans now know as the troubled Crown Heights section, home of racial and ethnic tensions.

The Jackie Robinson Ebbets Field Houses now stand where the ballpark was, and it's more than a little ironic, that this supposedly most progressive of all major league sporting franchises of the post-war period, abandoned the area which symbolizes the

61

racial tensions of the nineties for a city that featured the most destructive riots in modern history.

The Dodgers, lionized as "The Boys of Summer" years after they left, were a sportswriter's dream. Full of educated, accessible and quotable players, they enchanted New York. The Dodgers were busy winning pennants while the haughty Yankees were beating them in the World Series. The Giants, though they played in upper Manhattan, were sometimes the forgotten team. Winning an occasional pennant, and featuring arguably the game's most exciting player, Willie Mays, they played in the awful Polo Grounds, with short fences, well under 300 feet in left and right fields, and a center field fence nearly 500 feet.

When the Dodgers began looking for a new home, they originally thought of a home in downtown Brooklyn, several miles away. Years later, thumbing through one of my father's old Popular Science magazines, I was astounded to see drawings of the proposed ballpark. It was to be a retractable dome, the magazine said. I thought the dome had been invented in Houston in the sixties.

O'Malley would build the new park himself if the city gave him the land. They dallied, and after discussions were held about a park in Flushing Meadows, where Shea Stadium now stands, O'Malley made a similar deal with Los Angeles. I, being the loyal Brooklynite, had grown up thinking that O'Malley epitomized all evil, but a few years ago, a book was published on the Dodgers move west. It was balanced, and convinced me that O'Malley was simply trying to extract the best deal for himself. He was years ahead of his time in playing cities against each other, and New York, being one of the most bureaucratic of all cities, didn't take seriously the unspoken threat to move.

In Los Angeles, I found out, the deal struck was not universally welcomed. The City Council in a most narrow vote, approved the deal, and the Dodgers went west. They played four seasons in the Los Angeles Memorial Coliseum, occasionally drawing crowds of over 80,000, and once drawing over 90,000 fans for an exhibition game with the Yankees.

62

Meanwhile, the Giants were drawing poorly in the Polo Grounds, and Horace Stoneham, their owner had definitely decided to abandon New York. He thought of moving to the virgin territory of Minneapolis, home of his top minor league franchise. When O'Malley discovered this, he decided that it would be a shame to lose the lucrative rivalry between the Giants and Dodgers, and he set about to convince Stoneham to move to San Francisco.

The Giants announced their departure some weeks before the end of the 1957 season, but at season's end, the Dodgers still hadn't officially announced their plans. The less than naive knew they would go, and many feel that the feeling of bereavment following the Dodger's exit was the beginning of the end for major league baseball's run as America's sport of choice.

Seeing as how several years into their run the Mets had drawn more fans than the Dodgers ever had while playing more ineptly as the erstwhile Bums had, many could question that feeling. But, it's hard to argue with the fact that when the Dodgers and Giants left New York, Yankee attendance fell, in spite of continuing excellent teams.

The Dodgers were an immediate hit out west, and continue to be, thirty-five years later, one of the most profitable of all franchises. Dodger Stadium, built in 1962, but looking years younger is a reason way.

It's situated on a hill, a few minutes north of downtown, but once you arrive, you can't see any trace of the city. The neighborhood surrounding the ballpark doesn't seem to be the best, but fans are largely removed from it. The majestic San Gabriel Mountains loom in the distance, and it's almost always great weather. Yes, Dodger Stadium is advantaged in that it's treated more kindly by the weather than those ballparks in the East and Midwest, but old O'Malley knew what he was doing when he built the park himself. When the Dodgers want to make a change, they don't have to ask the city for permission. They've built a ballpark that seems both contemporary and out of place, just like Disneyland.

Fred Clare, the Dodgers' general manager, says in some ways, the Dodgers try to run their operation like Disney. "Come to Dodger Stadium, it's your stadium," he likes to say, just as they might at Disneyland. The Dodgers try to take care of the physical plant as religiously as do the Disney folks, and the fans seem to be well behaved, and not messy.

Clare believes that the team should sell baseball, not competitive or winning baseball, and though in 1992, the Dodgers finished last for the first time since 1905, they still drew nearly three million people. That great weather and fine stadium help, no doubt, but, the clever marketing obviously plays a part.

Dodger Stadium is symmetrical, with lots of foul ground, a feature of all the ballparks in California, and has older ushers, with straw hats, who have probably been there as long as the team has. Everyone is polite and helpful, and it's just a pleasure to watch a game there. The fans do leave early;there's no mass transportation, so everyone drives, and they don't see particularly enthusiastic, but they're loyal and pleasant.

In the winter of 1979, I visited California for the first time, and drove to Dodger Stadium, and through a pouring rainstorm, I walked inside, and briefly looked out on the park. I gasped. I had only been to a handful of parks then, but the light blue fences fit the setting so beautifully. I could only marvel, and each time I visit, I marvel yet again. It's so logical. It's thought out so well. There's little wrong with it. Sure, there's too much foul ground, but the Dodgers think of everything. They encourage celebrities to attend. Former players are welcomed, and the press is catered to nicely, as well.

In the early years at Dodger Stadium, B.W., that's Before Walkman, there were transistor radios, and thousands of Dodger fans brought their radios to listen to the heavenly Vin Scully. Scully is so good that many writers listen to him in the press box, something I've never seen anywhere else. His style is spare, and yet vivid. No one is as quick with a phrase, and they're not rehearsed.

Once at a post-season game, some walls holding up temporary

64

stands toppled. "It's like Jericho, and the walls came tumbling down," he remarked. Johnny Bench, who has worked several World Series with him on CBS radio says that Scully is so skilled that it always seems that he has already witnessed the game that's occuring before him as he describes it.

Several of his colleagues tell a story that Scully was once on the phone during an inning he wasn't broadcasting, his back to the field. He heard the roar of the crowd, hung up, and asked his partner to briefly fill him in. Seconds later, Scully was on the air expounding on a controversial and seldom seen play, as if he had seen it all. Witnesses say his description was so convincing you couldn't doubt he had seen it. Vin Scully is Dodger baseball.

There's Wrigley, there's Fenway, Yankee Stadium, too, there's Camden Yards now, and there's Dodger Stadium. It's in the pantheon of major league parks, and there it will stay as long as we both shall live.

Dodger Stadium was home of another major league club for several years. You've probably forgotten that the Angels played there. They didn't call it Dodger Stadium, they called it Chavez Ravine, after the area it was located in. When baseball expanded in 1961, and the Angels were admitted to the American League, they played in Wrigley Field, an authentic bandbox so small it was the home of the hokey television series, "Home Run Derby" around that time. You may have seen that old black and white series on ESPN, where the top sluggers in baseball participated in a home run hitting contest while between turns, they engaged in monosyllabic discussions with host Mark Scott.

Wrigley Field was modeled after the Chicago version, including ivy, and it was small. Located, not far from where Dodger Stadium now stands, it drew less than 600,000 fans in the Angels only season there.

In the mid-sixties, the Angels' own ballpark was built. Anaheim Stadium, near Disneyland, about thirty miles south of L.A. in Orange County, reminds one not of Dodger Stadium.

"Welcome to Anaheim Stadium," the parking lot attendant

smiles. "Welcome to Anaheim Stadium," the ticket seller remarks. "Welcome to Anaheim Stadium," the ticket taker intones. It's an okay place, but after three welcomes in five minutes, I was ready for some good eastern rudeness.

On my first visit, I asked a ticket seller for the best seat he had. It was for a box seat in lower right field. The large ballpark, which can seat over 60,000 was much more than half empty, and I was hoping for a better seat. I asked an usher near home plate if I might be able to sit there for a small fee. "Oh, we could get fired for taking a bribe. This isn't like those stadiums back east. This is Anaheim Stadium." I thought, he would get fired at those stadiums back east for not taking a bribe.

I've bribed a few ushers in my time, but having learned the trick of sitting quietly in a seat that's not yours, I'm reminded of my late great uncle, Fritz. He was barely five feet, and weighed less than one hundred pounds, and briefly was a matchmaker at several New York boxing clubs. For a time, he was a fare collector on New York trolley cars. To beat a fare, riders would often feign sleep or bury their heads in a newspaper. To thwart them, he would mark a small chalked "X" on the backs of those who paid their fare. When some fare beater protested they had already paid, Fritz would admonish them, "you don't have an 'X' on your back." Perhaps ushers should begin to carry chalk to prevent those who don't belong in seats from sneaking their way down.

Peter Schmuck, the baseball writer for The Baltimore Sun, and an Orange County native, remembers the atmosphere well. "My friend and I would see two good box seats that were empty, ask the guys who were using the other two if we could sit there, and they'd say sure. They'd buy us hot dogs, Cokes, souvenirs." When his young children become eleven or twelve, he wouldn't dream of allowing them to attend a game in Baltimore on their own, much less accept food from a stranger.

Another baseball writer in Baltimore, Joe Gross, sports editor of The Annapolis Capital, grew up in Philadelphia after World War II, and as a young child, would hop a street car and attend

66

Athletics games. The idea of allowing a seven-year-old to do that today is beyond the realm of our conception. Twice, Gross swears, a friendly old man bought him hot dogs at Shibe Park. When his father accompanied Joe to a later game, his son pointed out his benefactor. His father was astounded. The man who had befriended Joe was the owner-manager of the A's, Connie Mack. Perhaps that's why the team had to move to Kansas City, too many hot dogs bought for young fans by an owner who skimped on player development.

Exiting Interstate 5 for Anaheim Stadium, one drives past a series of "eighties" buildings. Those are the green, clear structures seen mostly in surburia and/or the Sun Belt that were built because the tax code encouraged it. When the tax laws ceased to encourage the construction of office buildings in 1986, those structures went out of vogue, and many are empty.

Lots of restaurants and hotels line the streets that border Anaheim Stadium, which is a bit of a surprise. You can actually walk to the ballpark from these places. For an effete easterner, it's always strange to find any type of "neighborhood" in Southern California, and especially strange around a ballpark. There's even an Amtrak stop at the park.

I spend lots of time riding trains on the East Coast, where cities are close together, and train travel is easy. If you visit Southern California, a wonderful train trip is from San Diego to Los Angeles, where you ride by the beach, and can detrain at Anaheim Stadium. It may remind you a bit of home.

The Angels' home is fairly antiseptic, seats mostly in orange, symmetrical, not much character, but not a bad place to watch a game. The fans aren't enthusiastic, but they're about the best behaved I've seen.

On my last visit, late in the 1992 season, in anticipation of watching George Brett attempt to swat his 3,000 hit, I happened on a game that lasted just one hour and forty-four minutes. This was the shortest game I could recall attending.

I hold the record for having attended the longest game in three parks: Memorial Stadium, refurbished Yankee Stadium, and

Three Rivers Stadium. In the Bronx, in 1976, I witnessed a 19 inning struggle against the Twins, where Gene Mauch, in an attempt to save with game, used five infielders and two outfielders for several batters in a late inning. It staved off defeat temporarily, but the Yankees eventually won. The Three Rivers game paradoxically was the first game I ever attended there, in 1989, an 18 inning game that began at 1:35, and complete with a rain delay, ended after 8 P.M.

Often, I moan that I'm a jinx; if I attend, surely a long game will follow. In the Orioles' first season in Camden Yards, I saw nearly half the games, but missed the longest.

George Brett was injured the night I was in Anaheim, but the next night he made four hits, the last of which was his 3000th. Besides seeing an extraordinarily snappy game, I nearly saw a perfect game. Kansas City's Dennis Rasmussen allowed just one baserunner, a single in the fourth inning, and the runner was immediately picked off. I have seen a no-hitter, Dave Righetti's Yankees against the Red Sox, on July 4, 1983, but never a perfect game. Rasmussen's artistry, facing the minimum 27 batters, was the closest I'd ever seen to perfection. The crowd that night was the smallest in more than a decade there, but true to their California roots, they began leaving after seven innings, with the game just about eighty minutes old.

Though some 17,000 tickets were sold, perhaps half that many were in attendance. There wasn't a threat of a traffic jam, and if they were worried about keeping their children up late, or having to rise early for work, why attend a night game anyway? Habits are hard to break, but it was absurd to see masses of people leave a game around nine o'clock. If the game had been a normal length game, (2 hours 50 minutes) they would have stayed for seven innings. They wouldn't have left after four innings. Wake up America, before it's too late.

South of Anaheim, it's baseball in paradise, San Diego. San Diego Jack Murphy Stadium, named after the late sportswriter for the San Diego Union, who tirelessly campaigned to bring major

68

league baseball to that city.

Hidden away at the intersection of two highways, it's not much to look at from the outside. It's just concrete, and it was built in the mid-sixties for both baseball and football. Sound familiar? Again, there's lots of foul ground, the seats aren't terribly close to the action, and the grass is lush.

It was the first major league park to sell sushi at a concession stand. (I wasn't brave enough to try it.) It also features the most healthful press room meals. One night, sea bass was on the menu, and the attendant made sure he portioned the proper amount of vegetables for me, as well as an attractive salad.

With some of the crowd coming from Mexico, Tijuana is about 15 miles south of San Diego, the Padres have some of their scoreboard listings in Spanish. When the Padres were admitted to the National League in 1969, they were far from an immediate commercial success. For many years, they regularly inhabited last place, and drew accordingly. After several years, the team was nearly sold and moved to Washington, D.C. The argument against baseball in San Diego was that it was competing against the Dodgers and Angels to the north, Mexico was to the south, the desert was to the east, and the Pacific ocean to the west.

After McDonald's magnate Ray Kroc bought the team, crowds picked up, and these days, there's no talk of moving. Besides, this place kind of reminds you of Dodger Stadium, in one way, anyway. There are hills outside the ballpark, in right field. Many relatively long-time San Diegans say that their city reminds them of what L.A. used to be like, 30 years ago, before all the growth. Isn't it funny that people who aren't native to an area, escape there to avoid the so-called sprawl, and then within several years of relocating, moan that the newcomers are spoiling it, and that their area isn't the way it used to be?

Padres fans don't like the Dodgers, they don't like L.A., and that makes for a nice rivalry. During the torrid 1991 Braves-Dodgers divisional race, Padre fans were openly rooting for

Atlanta. For those who thought that San Diegans couldn't get passionate about baseball, it was great to see otherwise.

The Padres' clubhouse was a quiet one, but for several seasons, the team was blessed by one of the wisest men in baseball, relief pitcher Larry Andersen. He's gone now, but I'll never forget a conversation we had. I heard he was a funny man, but he was seriously answering my questions. I challenged him to make me laugh.

Andersen: Is Miller Lite as a feather? I don't know what makes my mind think of stuff like that. I was sitting there, having a beer, and I'm thinking about why they call it light. They take 20 calories out of something, and all of a sudden, they call it light. There's some kind of chemical imbalance in my brain to let things like that come to mind.

Americans throw rice at weddings. Do Chinese throw hot dogs?

Dubroff: I was in Japan a few years ago, and I found out they don't eat hot dogs at ball games.

Andersen: Then, they're not ball games. You got to have hot dogs at ball games.

Dubroff: I never eat hot dogs at ball games.

Andersen: But, you're a vegetarian.

Dubroff: No, I like hamburgers.

Andersen: Ah, hamburgers are all right. I know you have a beer with them. Probably.

Dubroff: Not when I'm driving.

Andersen: You're not driving at the ballgame. You're just sitting there.

Dubroff: I'm driving afterwards.

Andersen: By that time, you should sober up. You watch us play some of our games, it'll sober anybody up.

I always wondered why blind people wear sunglasses. Do deaf people wear earmuffs?

Recently, I was in a delicatessen in Baltimore, and I thought of Larry Andersen. There was antipasto, put there wasn't any propasto. Say good night Gracie, it's time to go up to the Bay Area.

They're staying! That's the big news this winter in the Bay Area. I was visiting San Francisco the day baseball officially refused to allow the Giants to move to St. Petersburg, Florida. I suffered through my only case of food poisioning as I heard the news. I ate dungeness crab cakes for lunch, and afterward hoped that no visitor to Baltimore would succumb to salmonella after eating Maryland crab cakes.

I was watching the wires one afternoon at work when the news that the Giants were moving to the Suncoast Dome came across. Bob Lurie thought that then commissioner Fay Vincent had allowed him to sell the team to a group that would move the unloved bunch. Vincent claimed he merely granted the authorization for Lurie to explore a relocation.

The Giants had played at windy Candlestick Park for more than three decades, mostly in isolation. The park was considered one of baseball's worst, particularly at night, for winds made conditions more suitable for the Idiatrod dog races than for the national pastime of the lower 48. For some years, the Giants had attempted to convince the public to finance a new home for them. Two attempts were made by the city of San Francisco to build a new downtown stadium. The last one, in 1989, was understandably, narrowly defeated in an Election Day referendum, by a queasy public, several weeks after the earthquake. Subsuquent attempts in Santa Clara County, and by the city of San Jose, were also defeated, and not long after the San Jose setback, plans for the move were announced.

Veterans recalled the late Horace Stoneham's remarks upon the Giants' departure from New York. When the owner was asked if he did not feel some measure of sympathy for the children who rooted for the Giants, he said he did, but he hadn't seen many of their fathers patronizing the ballpark recently.

Public demonstrations to show their support for the Giants were organized by The City, as it likes to call itself, but with gatherings of just several hundred, in many cases, it was assumed that people in San Francisco simply didn't care if the team departed.

The Giants supposed final game in San Francisco was an almost sell-out in late September, but quietly a deal was hammered out where some local business leaders underbid the Floridians by an estimated $10 million, and left the Tampa Bay Area jealous of the San Francisco Bay Area. (In truth, I've long felt the west coast of Florida deserved a team, and was surprised the National League chose Miami as its Sunshine State expansion representative.)

After the team changed hands, the Giants made a clumsy, though successful effort to snare free agent Barry Bonds. (The deal was temporarily held hostage as then owner of record Bob Lurie said he would not guarantee Bonds' contract should the sale of the team not be approved. It was.) The new owners of the team made plans to make plans to build a new stadium, and to make over the old stadium in the interim.

Candlestick Park is located at Candlestick Point at the southern end of San Francisco. When driving into the city, oops, I'm sorry, The City, from the airport, there the park is, looking out at the clear blue water. From a distance, the park looks sort of modern, like lots of the others I've seen, circular and concrete, but come on inside.

It's most unusual, like The City it's a part of. The major league's only swinging doors, painted a bright drab, lead you from the concourse to the stands. One can only assume that the doors are supposed to keep wind away. The bullpens are on the field, and are painted similarly drab. The visitor's dugout, on the third base side, is an orphan. The visitor's clubhouse is located down the right field line, behind the bullpen, and after a pitcher is removed from a game, he sits in his dugout until the completion of the inning. Then, he trudges past the Giant dugout, so that he can be jeered by some of baseball's rowdiest fans. Chic San Franciscans don't attend baseball games. They don't hang out in Hunters Point, the decidedly unchic neighborhood Candlestick Park is located in.

72

Perhaps they root for the 49rs, but not for the Giants.

It's been a puzzle to me why so few residents of a city actually attend games played in their cities. Baseball is more of a suburban game now, it seems, with Wrigley Field, and its neighborhood yuppies, when was the last time you heard that term, being an exception. The neighborhood around Wrigley is a fashionable one, and many residents do attend.

Though at some ballparks, you do get a sense of what city you're in, at many you don't, and while the atmosphere differs from park to park, I don't that stadiums take on the characteristics of the city that they're located in. Sure, patrons at Shea or Yankee Stadiums may be more arrogant than those in Kansas City, the stadiums themselves, unless one can readily see the skyline, wouldn't necessarily clue an alien into what city they had landed in.

San Francisco is a great walking city, hills and all. Besides the touristy cable cars, there are lots of buses, light rail, and the BART. Except for some buses, mass transit is useless at Candlestick Park. The BART doesn't come close, and a cab ride from a downtown hotel, complete with a driver complaining about the cheap ballplayers he just had in his cab can run one nearly twenty dollars, and try and find one after the game!

A new downtown stadium in San Francisco would be lovely, but night games would still be cold, though perhaps not as cold as at Candlestick. Fans who brave the elements and sat through an extra inning night game receive Croix De Candlestick, a pin with a frost tinged S.F., and the words, "Vendi, Vidi, Vici." It translates, "I came, I saw, I conquered."

Across the Bay, perhaps fifteen miles away, sits the Oakland-Alameda County Coliseum, home of the Oakland Athletics, one of the most successful franchishes in baseball.

When Charles O. Finley moved the A's from Kansas City for the 1968 season, he brought the Bay Area a second team, and though the club was baseball's finest for a few years, few cared. Finley didn't promote much, and the team had trouble drawing a million. When free agency came, the undercapitalized Finley was unprepared, and he began shedding players. In 1979, just five years after the team won its third consecutive world's championship, the A's lost 108 games and drew about 300,000 fans for the <u>entire</u> season. After Finley sold the club during the 1980 season, the team became more competitive under Billy Martin, and in 1990, they drew nearly ten times as many fans as they had in 1979.

It was argued during the A's heyday of the seventies that people in the Bay Area just wouldn't support two teams. There wasn't that much interest in the sport. In the sixties in Chicago, they used to say the same about professional baseketball.

When the Haas family bought the A's, and began intelligently marketing the club, attendance took off. The A's were the first to offer baby changing stations in their bathrooms. They were also the first team in an outdoor stadium to ban smoking, except on the concourse, and they were one of the first teams to offer a variety of foods for sale. Their selection of music is creative, and the sound system is an inoffensive one.

These qualities are all important because the stadium is one of the most boring physically in the game. It's perfectly symmetrical, there's more foul ground here than anywhere else in baseball, and it's probably the least intimate stadium in the show.

Located hard by a working class neighborhood in Oakland, it's easily reached by BART. Once inside, a fan wouldn't know they were near inner city Oakland. The BART ride to the park from San Francisco, or the East Bay takes you past lots of factories, gas stations and modest housing. The ride isn't one you would imagine taking in Northern California, but can remind you of one you might take from the Loop to Comiskey Park, through the near South Side.

With lush greens and wide concourses past the outfield wall, and the Oakland hills lurking in the background, it's pleasant California, a much more pleasant experience than Candlestick. During a rare doubleheader at Candlestick, I went from shirt to sweater to shirt, back to sweater, to jacket in the space of a few innings. In Oakland, with the temperature in the high sixties, this eastern boy had forgotten that sun burns are possible, and I suffered the consequences one afternoon.

Sitting in the upper deck, soaking in the sun, watching a game in Oakland, I appreciated the art of promotion. In California, there are so many other things to do besides watch a baseball game on a spring or summer afternoon in the weekend, and if the Giants can promote nearly as well as the Dodgers or A's have, perhaps even chic San Fransicans will make their way to a ballgame once in a while. They do serve wine at Candlestick, but the only cheese came with burgers or nachos. If they start serving tofu, I may have to switch to football.

Chapter 8:

Cotton-Eyed Joe

By the time you read this, he won't be pitching any longer. He'll not pitch in the new ballpark in Arlington. He's just getting too old, he says. He's less than ten years older than I am, but he's lost some of his hair, and a yard off his fastball. They're going to have a new ballpark in Arlington, and they need one, but I'm sorry you didn't see the old one.

It was what they like to call a throwback. Located in Arlington, about two-thirds of the way between Dallas and Fort Worth, they played minor league ball there for years. They called it Turnpike Stadium, because it was, you guessed it, just off the turnpike. Now, it's called Arlington Stadium, and it's across that turnpike, or the highway, from Six Flags Over Texas.

It's hotter there than anywhere else in big league ball. It's so hot that the Rangers play only a handful of afternoon games all season. Long before ESPN, the Rangers regularly hosted Sunday Night Baseball.

During the years the Rangers have played at Arlington Stadium, they've never hosted an All-Star or post season game, and except for that great old guy, Nolan Ryan, they really haven't attracted much national attention.

The old park has a higher percentage of seats in fair territory than at any other yard, but if you're fortunate enough to sit in foul territory, you may have one of the better seats in big league baseball.

Television is such a liar. You can't tell much about a ballpark from TV. Arlington looked so sterile for all those years on the tube, but if you're sitting by the bases, you're very close to the field. The folks there are friendly, and if you like nachos, you've come to the right place. Seemingly hundreds of trays of nachos stacked on top of each other in concession stands, and they looked fresh, too. Lots of hamburgers, and they tasted good, too. They have Blue Bell ice cream, Texas' own, in the narrow concourses, and the bathrooms are down in the bowels of the stadium, through some dark passageways.

For a visiting writer on deadline, it's not so charming. Take the elevator, or walk down from the press box to the field, fight your way past thousands of exiting fans, walk through the stands onto the field, through the dugout, and a dank, dark tunnel until you reach the clubhouse.

Once you're there, you don't have to worry about players rushing to catch the bus. Most teams stay at the Arlington Sheraton, a long fly ball, as they say, from the park, in deep left field. (The new park is adjacent to the old one.)

Players walk to the park from the hotel. Instead of arriving three hours before a game, as they would at home, in Texas, many come in the early afternoon. Other than Six Flags and a few decent Mexican restaurants a short drive away, there's not much to do in Arlingon, anyway, and Dallas is a good forty-five minutes away.

Autograph hounds permeate the perimeter of the hotel. The management of the Sheraton has banned loitering, but these kids are more polite than the ones who stand in front of the Westin in Chicago or the Grand Hyatt in New York.

When the Washington Senators relocated in 1972, baseball was a hard sell in the Metroplex, as they refer to the Dallas-Fort Worth area. Football was the favorite sport, and by August, the newspapers are full of news not only about the Cowboys, but about the Southwest Conference schools, and even high schools, too. Baseball is a distant second.

The fans aren't terribly knowledgable, but they aren't annoying. They're pretty passive, except at seventh inning stretch time. Instead of "Take Me Out to the Ball Game," a vaguely familiar tune loudly drifted out of the public address system. Fiddling sounds, whoops and foot stomps from the crowd. It was that old Texas favorite "Cotton-Eyed Joe," and I was charmed by the fans whistling, hooting and hollering.

In the these days of Holiday Inns, McDonald's, recorded wake-up calls and MTV, here was something different.

By the time you read this, old Nolan Ryan will be gone, so will Arlington Stadium, but I hope not "Cotton-Eyed Joe."

Chapter 9:
Don't Give Up on the Tig-uhs

If you ask the overwhelming majority of baseball fans what they remember about Carlton Fisk's home run in the sixth game of the 1975 World Series, it's doubtful they would be able to name the announcer who described it on NBC.

If you tell that to the announcer who called the home run, Dick Stockton, who now broadcasts baseball for the Oakland A's, he'll ask, "Do you remember who called Bobby Thomson's home run on television?" I quickly answered "Ernie Harwell," and as my prize, got to spend a day with Stockton and his partner, Jim Kaat, in the CBS booth watching them broadcast an Orioles-Red Sox contest. Actually, even if I didn't know it was Harwell, Stockton would have invited me, but it sounds better this way.

For more than forty years, fans have seen the grainy films of Thomson circling the bases, with the voice of Russ Hodges screaming, "The Giants win the pennant!" over and over. They don't realize that Hodges broadcast the game on the radio, and that there's not a sound track for the television picture. That's too bad, both for history's sake, and for Ernie Harwell's sake.

"The only people who remember" that he was the announcer for that historic game were "Mrs. Harwell and me," he likes to joke, and while Stockton's call has been obscured by the image of Fisk waving that home run fair, I had the good fortune to visit with both of these men within a few days of each other.

I've always had a fascination with broadcasters. I've been in broadcasting for more than fifteen years, and as a small boy, at night, I'd listen to broadcasts of games I could receive on the radios my grandfather had given me. He was a radio and television repairman, and his old radios could receive games from Philadelphia, Boston, Baltimore and Chicago, when the weather was right. It was a great way to learn baseball, geography and broadcasting.

When NBC owned the exclusive rights to the World Series for eons, there was a charming custom. Besides using the regular NBC crew for the series, each team's lead broadcaster would announce their home games nationally along with Curt Gowdy and Tony Kubek. It gave the fans around the country an opportunity to see Vin Scully when the Dodgers were in the Series, or Harry Caray when the Cardinals were, or Dick Stockton, in his first year as a Red Sox announcer. As Harwell points out, when baseball had just one national telecast a week, the Saturday game of the week, and you saw Gowdy and Kubek week in and week out, seeing the local broadcasters gave the telecast the feel of something different, something special. The local men were also much more knowledgable about the teams, and in those pre-cable, pre-USA Today days, often able to add something about the players that wasn't generally known to the public. I well recall New York Mets announcer LIndsey Nelson telling America during the 1973 World Series about a slouching, free spirited, seldom used Met outfielder's unusual gait. Of George Theodore, he said, "He runs like Groucho Marx." Though, as a New Yorker, I had heard him say that during the year, he was able to succintly inform the rest of America that they were watching a different kind of player.

When ABC began alternating coverage of the Series with NBC in 1977, the local announcers disappeared, and some of the fun of the Series was gone too, for the announcers, and for the viewers.

Stockton, who from 1990-1992 generally called the "back-up" game that is shown in a smaller region than the primary game, broadcasts several sports for CBS, and he's not like Harwell, or Jon Miller, or Vin Scully, known primarily as a baseball man. In fact, as the play-by-play man for the NBA for many years, he's probably best known for helping make that league.

Stockton's favorite sport is "whatever I'm doing. If I'm doing baseball, it's baseball. Fans like different sports. I like different sports." He allows that the pace of a baseball game enables him to have more a sense of humor than on other sports, and that he can have a chat with the viewer, and be more conversational. "In football, you have bursts," he explains, "and then, the analysts talk." In basketball, "you're just putting captions on pictures. All you have time to say is 'And the Pistons are up by five.'"

Baseball is more relaxing to prepare for than football. The pre-game ritual for football is rigid, "militaristic," where the announcers spend a twelve hour day preparing for a telecast. "I'm almost exhausted at the end of the day before a game," and he says that it's easier broadcasting the game than preparing for it.

On the day that he had generously invited me to join him and Kaat in the booth for, Stockton was anything but relaxed. Both men were sweating profusely, as the temperature reached 99 degrees during the game. Stockton intently watched the action on the field as well as the monitors in front of him while his statistical assistant, Marty Aronoff, fed him information to help identify pitchers warming up in the bullpen, or pinch hitters. Aronoff would also help him keep the ball and strike count so that Stockton could listen to Kaat's comments and the directions from the producer and director in CBS' truck.

Stockton and Kaat had only worked together for perhaps twenty-five games in two seasons by the time I caught up with them, a short time in baseball television, but they obviously enjoyed working together, though Stockton says that's not a necessity. Some play-by-play men like to ask questions of their analysts, Stockton doesn't. "I don't ask questions. I enjoy the back and forth" between commentator and play-by-play broadcaster. Unlike others, Stockton is adamant about preferring television. "I love television. Given the choice, who doesn't want to see it? I have no problems with television." Who'll remember a radio description of Roger Clemens arguing with home plate umpire Terry Cooney in the 1990 American League Championship Series, but who'll forget the picture? Stockton and Kaat won't; they called that game for CBS.

Stockton's model broadcaster? "Pat Summerall. Pat's the model" in being able to pithily describe action on the field and setting up his long-time sidekick, John Madden. Stockton says that Summerall and Madden are not personally close, but they're a beautiful team, and he tried to emulate their work with Kaat.

83

While Stockton is intense, Kaat is a bit looser. He watches the action standing on one foot, with the other perched on the table near his monitor. Stockton stayed put, and remained focused, except for briefly joshing with Aronoff.

Stockton adeptly played straight man as the two discussed the new stadium then being built in Baltimore. "When you have a chance to name a park Camden Yards, you take it," he offered, and to Kaat, he slyly asked, "In Nashville, what was the name of the park where you played, Sulphur Dell?" Left unsaid was the feeling a viewer had of, boy, I sure would have liked to have seen what Sulphur Dell looked like. He also left unsaid the fact that there were many Memorial Stadiums around America, but only one Sulphur Dell.

Unlike Stockton, most of the great broadcasters who've worked both television and radio prefer the latter. "It's more of an art form," the Phillies long-time voice, Harry Kalas, maintains, though most do the bulk of their work on television for the money and exposure. Though Scully also prefers radio, as Stockton points out, "The guys who say they prefer radio," particularly Scully, make certain they're amply exposed on the tube. When the Dodgers televise an away game, Scully calls the firsst three and last three innings alone on television, and the middle three innings alone on radio, an arrangement not found elsewhere in baseball. A popular story, told to me by several broadcasters, was that Scully, when working NFL games on CBS, actually demanded to work games without an analyst, an unheard of scenario in contemporary television.

While Scully, Miller, Caray and Jack Buck all work games on radio and television, it's interesting to note that only Caray will say that he prefers working on television.

Stockton is a professional sports broadcaster, claiming no loyalty to a particular sport, Jon Miller and Ernie Harwell are baseball all the way. Though Miller has broadcast some football, basketball and soccer, he's a baseball man.

Miller works both television and radio for the Orioles, and though he prefers radio, he's great on the tube, too. Working with Jim Palmer on a game from decrepit Cleveland Stadium one night, he commented on a long foul ball that Cal Ripken had sent high into the empty expanse of the upper left field stands. "There hasn't been a ball hit there since 1317, since the Crusades," Miller remarked, and you had to laugh aloud.

He doesn't look right wearing a jacket and tie to the park. One the nights he's on the radio, he's apt to arrive with his bulging briefcase several hours before gametime. Besides the press guides, newspapers, field glasses and scorebook, he places an egg timer at his broadcast position. That's a reminder for him to give the score every three minutes. His ballpark attire can be described as eccentric. On a hot summer evening, instead of an Izod shirt with slacks and loafers, he's liable to be found in an Hawaiian shirt, shorts and rubber flip-flops.

At forty-one, the recognized premiere broadcaster of his generation, Miller is renowned for his impersonations of other broadcasters such as Caray, Buck and Scully, but his style is unique--sort of Milleresque. Voice rising at exciting moments, when an Oriole would double with the bases loaded, driving in three runs, he'll boom, "And they All score!" When the Orioles draw even with an opponent, he'll yell, "and it's all tied up!"

Miller broke into the major leagues at twenty-two, about average for a player, quite young for a broadcaster. He was hired by that astute judge of broadcasting talent, Charles O. Finley. A year, later, he was fired by that same astute judge of broadcasting talent. Born eight days after Bobby Thomson's historic home run, Miller, grew up in the San Francisco Bay Area, fantasizing about being a broadcaster for a big league team. He was worried as a teenager that he wouldn't be afforded the opportunity, let alone for his home town team striving for its third consecutive championship.

"When I was a kid, I kept thinking the game was heading for a fall, and I was hoping I'd be able to get hired to broadcast big league baseball before it was extinct. We've all gotten a little more sophisticated. All these things happened, and the game's gotten stronger."

Working for Finley was a unique experience. "I'd call him up, and I'd say, 'Mr. Finley?' 'Alive and breathing, alive and speaking, now what do you want?'" Finley would reply.

Finley's A's, despite having won two consecutive worlds championships, and on the way to their third, drew about 810,000 fans in Miller's year, 1974. That figure was inflated by the half-price ticket promotion Finley initiated for Monday night games halfway through the season.

In the playoffs, the A's played the Orioles, who also failed to draw a million despite many years of consistently outstanding teams. That's unthinkable today, when even an occasional minor league team draws a million. The increased interest in the game, which Miller attributes to the excitement of the 1975 World Series, has made baseball a healthier game than ever.

Much of the resurgence can be credited to the greater emphasis on offense. The Reds and Red Sox were full of great hitters, and after watching some years of little offense, fans, and newer fans, welcomed the scoring. With the Red Sox, and the Yankees featuring great hitting in the mid and late seventies, baseball was back. Free agency has been a boon, too. "The winter time is filled with baseball news," he observes. In 1985, for example, the Orioles, for the first time, spent heavily, and as it turned out, unwisely on free agents. The club "obliterated all their attendance records, and they were never in the pennant race," Miller points out. "Did it pay off? People showed up."

With fantasy leagues popular, many books catering to the need for statistical information have been published, and he compares these days to his 1974 rookie year. "What a guy hit against lefties, what he hit against righties, what he hit against different pitchers, this was anybody's guess. The teams themselves had this info, but they called them intelligence reports, and they were guarded like classified documents. I couldn't get a copy of the Oakland A's intelligence reports. I was only allowed to look at them while I was in the offices. I wasn't to reveal to anyone what this thing said," he cracked in mock seriousness. Today, before every game, uniform, detailed statistics, courtesy of IBM, are available along press row.

After his rookie year, Miller was let go, but then again, so were twelve others before him. To hire Miller, Finley had dismissed Jim Woods, who had ably broadcast baseball for a number of big league teams. Miller, despite his short tenure, regards the experience as a great one because he could ask Alvin Dark, the A's manager, lots of stupid questions, and he'd get intelligent answers. The A's played excellent defense, threw to the correct base, pitched and hit well, and had no visible weaknesses. They also had many outstanding and colorful ballplayers. He learned more in his first year as a big league broadcaster with the A's than he would have learned as a minor league broadcaster, or even with a less skilled major league team.

Miller had taken a tape recorder to Candlestick Park, and called a game. He sent the tape to the A's, and Monte Moore, long-time A's voice, liked it, and played it for Finley over the telephone. Miller was hired, and fired after one year, shortly before spring training began in 1975. At a baseball writer's banquet in Chicago, Bob Waller, unemployed after being dismissed by the White Sox at the end of the previous season, was accosted by Finley. Waller was offered--and accepted the A's job after Finley told him he had to decide on the offer immediately so that Finley could announce it to the crowd. Waller didn't last long, and Miller says that in any event, he would have been bounced a season or two later, anyway.

Miller, who also broadcast games in Texas and Boston, says his preparation is on-going, reading a number of newspapers and keeping up with the news. Reading box scores is vital, but Miller hopes not to need much of what he has read. "You hope it's such a good game that you have all you can handle just keeping up with the game. If the game itself is not interesting, then you need things to make the broadcast interesting."

Miller clearly prefers radio, where the broadcast is his. Everything (on radio) is built upon the play-by-play man's sense of timing, sensibility, and feel for the game. Television is very collaborative; you have the producer, director, the analyst who are all having their input on what's important at the moment. Very often, you're just trying to provide the proper caption for the picture that's up, and to provide the space for the analyst to do his thing. Radio's a lot more fun because it's your deal. Television is everybody's deal."

Ernie Harwell is the most prominent contemporary announcer known for working on radio. Though in 1992, after his dismissal by the Detroit Tigers, he worked some telecasts for the California Angels, he hadn't worked on television in more than a generation.

In his early years with the Tigers, he was on both radio and television, but in the mid-sixties, the games began being sponsored by competing breweries: Stroh's for radio and Pabst for television. Harwell had been associated with Stroh's for many seasons, and it was mandated that he stay with them.

"If I had a choice, I'd rather be on TV at least some," he admitted in mid-1991, citing the money and exposure television brings. "Radio is more fun. The announcer's a bigger guy on the radio. We don't have to worry what a producer or director wants us to say. You can use you full range of description. You use the imagination of the listener on the radio. TV is sort of a peep show; the best thing that ever happened for television was replay." Harwell does watch games on television, but listens to the radio broadcast with the television sound muted, when a broadcast is available.

With television, "you have to concentrate a lot, you have to sit there, and you have to sort of watch it because a good television announcer doesn't say a whole lot. On radio, we have to repeat and repeat and repeat. My philosophy is that when people listen to a radio broadcast, they don't listen very carefully. They're doing other things. The announcer should be a scene setter from time to time, and keep setting the scence. I try to keep it as simple as I can. If I try to get too fancy, I fall all over myself," he confesses.

The Tig-_uhs_, as Harwell would say, fell all over themselves when they foolishly announced during the off-season that the 1991 season would be the 73-year old Harwell's last. Bo Schembechler, the club's president, who would be fired in August 1992, took the blame initially, but later officials of WJR, the Tigers' flagship station, insisted it had been their idea. The reaction around Michigan was overwhelmingly negative, and among Ernie's friends and admirers around baseball, it was one of disgust. No one felt the firing was justified, and it received much national attention.

Harwell is such a genuinely nice, warm and approachable man that it was difficult for me to ask him about his firing. "I know you've been asked this a million times, and I feel guilty asking you this," I began. "Don't feel guilty, go ahead," he said, and finally, I asked how he felt about this ultimate insult.

"I was surprised. I thought I'd work a couple of more years, and then I would retire." He had contemplated retiring, but by the time he was informed of the team's plans, it was relatively late to begin a job search. He didn't want to leave the Tigers, liked living in Michigan, liked the money, and shockingly, wasn't at all certain another team would want him.

After the 1991 season, besides signing to broadcast some Angels games, he signed a two-year contract with CBS radio to broadcast games each Saturday.

The Tigers didn't realize that Harwell's firing would be a national cause celebre, one that even embarrassed Harwell. On working his lame duck season he said, "It's sort of embarrassing that I'm working for people that have told me they don't want me back."

Ernie Harwell and Tiger Stadium represented the old in Detroit. The Tigers wanted a new image, but perhaps they should have kept in mind the Cubs and Harry Caray. Wrigley and Caray are of the same vintage as Tiger Stadium and Harwell, but while Tiger Stadium is outdated, and Wrigley isn't, Caray is celebrated by the ballclub and its fans. Harwell is as big a man in Detroit as Caray is in Chicago, though he was rudely dismissed by the team he has spent more than three decades selling. A team's announcers are its principal salesman, and though Tiger attendance has lagged, his enthusiasm and skills are still nonpareil. Did the Tigers ever think that maybe they were at fault?

Nevertheless, he was still a Tiger fan. I'd told him my in-laws, who lived not far from Harwell in suburban Detroit, were disgusted with the treatment he received. He was appreciative, and after we concluded and shook hands, he said, "Tell your relatives in Livonia not to give up on the Tig-uhs" even though they'd given up on him.

As the season progressed, and the ballclub unexpectedly challenged for the American League East title, I kept hoping the team would admit its error and bring Ernie back. He wasn't sure if he still wanted to work, but this legend deserved the opportunity to decide for himself. "I think maybe there'd be somebody who'd give me a job," he thought. In the end, he had two part-time jobs for 1992. "It keeps me out of trouble," he observed.

When the Tigers were sold during the 1992 season, their new owner, Mike Ilitch decided that maybe Ernie could come back, and call a few innings during each game in 1993. Don't give up on the Tig-uhs.

Chapter 10:

Two Homes of the Braves

For half a century, until 1953, baseball had sixteen teams in just ten cities in America. Three in New York, two each in Chicago, Boston, Philadelphia and St. Louis, and single franchises in Washington, Cincinnati, Cleveland, Detroit and Pittsburgh.

After World War II, the country's population began to shift, and baseball's owners began to get impatient. Expansion was nearly a decade away, and only agreed to because Branch Rickey attempted to organize a third major league, the Continental League in 1959. The proposed league, with eight teams, was stillborn, but it accomplished its major goal, which was to return a second team to New York.

The first team to move in more than fifty years was the Boston Braves. Long considered the second team in Boston, they played at Braves Field, a few miles from Fenway Park. Today, Boston University plays its football games on the same site, and it's called Nickerson Field.

When the Braves decided to move to Milwaukee for the 1953 season, a jubilant city awaited them. For the balance of the decade, the Braves set attendance records, and even managed to beat the Yankees in a World Series. The following year, they took the Yankees to a seventh game before losing. Seemingly the entire state of Wisconsin loved the Braves who played in County Stadium, but the love affair was fleeting, and barely a dozen years after arriving in Milwaukee, they were on their way to Atlanta, to become the southeast's first professional sports team.

Though Milwaukee had become relatively apathetic towards the Braves, they fought hard to keep them, but the National League, in a case forcefully argued in court by their lawyer, Bowie Kuhn, won, and in 1966, for the first time, a major league franchise had moved twice. Two years later, the Philadelphia-Kansas City-Oakland Athletics could make the same dubious boast.

91

The Braves had some great players: Hank Aaron, Eddie Mathews and Warren Spahn. Mathews played in all three cities, Aaron didn't play in Boston, and Spahn didn't play in Atlanta. Spahn managed to begin his career playing for Boston Braves manager Casey Stengel, and end it playing for Stengel in New York, leading Spahn to claim that he had played for Stengel both before and after he was designated a genius.

Despite the presence of Aaron, Phile Niekro, Dale Murphy and other fine players, the Braves didn't win a post season game until 1991. Atlanta was terribly apathetic towards the team for many years. During one of its particularly dreary seasons, Braves announcer Skip Caray surveyed yet another crowd of several thousand and drolly observed that Atlanta Fulton-County Stadium was the scene of "another partial sell-out."

Today, it's different. After years in the wilderness, the Braves became sudden contenders in 1991, and tickets became scarce commodities. The Braves' attendance, a few years before the lowest in the National League, was now the highest, and with the major's best pitching, and a farm system stocked with excellent young talent, the outlook for partial sell outs was happily dim.

Back in the sixties, a young partial Milwaukeean was upset that his team was leaving town. Bud Selig dedicated himself to bringing baseball back to Milwaukee. He was able to convince the Chicago White Sox to play a handful of games in Milwaukee in the interim, and by 1970, baseball was back in cheese land.

Kansas City and Seattle were granted expansion franchises by the American League in 1969, and after one season in dreary Sicks Stadium, the Seattle Pilots, nearly bankrupt, were sold to Selig, and just before the start of the 1970 season, were moved and renamed the Milwaukee Brewers.

The Brewers are the epitome of what baseball calls a small market team. With Chicago to the south, Lake Michigan to the east, and some medium sized cities to its north and west, the Brewers' drawing area is a small one, perhaps the most restricted in the game. At least San Diego has Mexico to draw from, but the Brewers must work hard to draw two million fans annually.

They put on a nice show in Milwaukee. County Stadium is located about ten minutes west of downtown in a lovely residential neighborhood. It reminded me of the neighborhood around Memorial Stadium, though this being the Midwest, the houses seemed larger. The stadium was built around the same time as Memorial Stadium, and its lower deck and outfield seating made me think I could be back in Baltimore. Its vast upper deck reminded me more of Cleveland.

When I first visited County Stadium, it was early September, and the Brewers were out of contention. The night was mild, sunset was still some time away, and I didn't need a jacket.

The crowd was under ten thousand. Back home, that no longer happened. (For years, in the American League, tickets sold were counted while in the National League, only those physically in attendance were reported. For the 1993 season, the National adopted the American's counting methods.) Often, I'd see a crowd announced at 25,000 in Memorial Stadium after a long rain delay when perhaps a third of that were actually attending. The Brewers' season ticket base was one of the lowest in baseball, and they had one of the smallest television contracts, with little revenue from local cable. But, they did have Bob Uecker calling their games.

When the cab pulled up by the ticket window ninety minutes before game time, the gates were about to open. I announced to the underworked ticket seller that I should like the best single seat he had for sale. After all, I hadn't been to County Stadium before. "Why the hell not?," the ticket salesman snarled, and smiled as he sold me one of the best seats in the park. Just two rows from the field, halfway between home plate and third base, near the visiting dugout.

I began watching batting practice, and after a few minutes, I roamed the stadium's concourses. In brown brick, it looked more like the halls of a pre-war high school with trophy cases full of athletic trophies that have lost their luster, and the quiet concourses were filled with interesting food stands.

Before entering the park, I had noticed a few hardy souls

grilling their bratwurst in the parking lot. Tailgating is
generally a football phenomenon, but in Milwaukee, I learned they
did it for baseball, too.

There were lots of German sausages available in the Brewers
brat house. Besides avoiding hot dogs, I don't care much for
sausage, but my spies tell me that the Brewers' wurst is the best.
Their cheeseburgers, and french fries were excellent for ball park
fare, and their ice cream, served in a bakery by middle aged women
in authentic starched bakery outfits, was good, too. It brought
back memories of walking several blocks each Saturday, to Leon's
on Knapp Street in Brooklyn, and buying a seeded rye bread for my
mother from the spiritual cousins of these women in County Stadium.
There is something to be said for having a major league franchise
in the middle of a dairy state.

Inside, my seat was close to the field, and other seats seemed
fairly intimate, too. The field was grass, and lots of beer vendors
were present, but thankfully, no drunkards. Despite an overly loud
public address system, the stadium experience was quite a pleasant
one.

On my first visit, I was engaged in conversation with a Robert
H. Milbourne, who turned out to be the President of the Greater
Milwaukee Committee. He attempts to promote business in Milwaukee,
and told me of the efforts to build a new stadium there.

County Stadium has no luxury boxes, and since the Brewers'
revenue base is a limited one, in order to compete, they must try
to make money where they can. A new stadium, with luxury boxes
would help, and plans are for one to be built adjacent to County
Stadium, just as is the case in Arlington.

In the succeeding years after my first visit, I found there
were two major problems in building the new stadium. The first was
that the environmentalists objected, saying that an ancient rock
base would be destroyed in the building of a new structure. The
second was that corporate Milwaukee suffered from a case of
relative disinterest. Fortunately, the tree huggers were either
assauged or avoided, and with Milbourne's help, another condition

was met: rental on most of the luxury boxes was committed to before construction began.

Milwaukee is a quiet big city. Stuck in Chicago's shadow, it's come to national news attention just once in recent memory. That's when Jeffrey Dahmer decided to become a degenerate mass murderer. Otherwise, the city lives, seemingly happily, in the background. Some of the lakefront houses resemble Chicago's, but downtown is quiet and subdued, unlike its brassy neighbors. If you've never visited Milwaukee, and you desire to, and you happen to be in Chicago, why don't you take the train?

Regular Amtrak service is available, and it's inexpensive, too. Riding north from Chicago, prosperous Lake County suburbs are viewed, and dairy farms come along a little later. The Wisconsin state prison comes next, with a John Deere factory, and then industrial Milwaukee. The ballpark is just a short cab ride away, and the hacks are friendly. They'll often have the post-game show on the radio, so you can hear Bob Uecker. By the way, he usually plays it straight for the locals, and if you're lucky, you may get to sit near Bob Milbourne, too. He's a friend of Bud Selig, and he's a friendly guy, a good guy to know. Selig gave him a most valuable card. It reads "Admit Robert Milbourne and a guest to any American League park."

They do play "Take Me Out to the Ball Game" in Milwaukee. But, they follow it with a rousing version of "The Beer Barrel Polka," straight from 1954's "Your Hit Parade," and while it's no "Cotton-Eyed Joe," it isn't half bad. Neither is County Stadium.

95

Before one Sunday afternoon game, I was walking towards the Brewer dugout. A civilian had his arm on top of the dugout. A child, perhaps eleven or twelve espied the arm from his perch in back of the dugout. As I neared the dugout, the child shrieked: "Who is that? Who is that?" I knew it was a sportswriter, but I paused, looked up at the child and replied: "It's Ernest Hemingway." The child immediately shouted: "Ernest, can I have your autograph, please?"

When I first visited Atlanta-Fulton County Stadium in the middle eighties, I was not impressed. Too much foul ground, the seats are too far from the field, the food was awful, and the stadium had no character.

I have been there many times since, and it's amazing how good teams playing in front of large crowds can lend a stadium character. When the Braves played before throngs of several thousand just a few years ago, it was hard to imagine that that some of the most exciting baseball in recent years would be played there.

When the Braves moved to Atlanta to become the city's first professional sports team, it was a town on the move. Dubbed as "the city too busy to hate," when the Braves began losing, it had a population that was too busy to attend baseball games. But when the team's fortunes reversed suddenly in 1991, the crowds came.

Atlanta-Fulton County Stadium is just about a mile from downtown. The streets aren't inviting; there's no direct way to the ballpark. You might want to walk past Georgia State University, and past the State Capitol building and Grady Hospital, but it's not an inspiring walk, as the ones to Fenway Park or Camden Yards might be.

It's one of those boring circular structures, built for baseball and football, though the Falcons moved to the nearby Georgia Dome for the 1992 season. If you sit by the window when you're flying in or changing planes at Hartsfield, you'll see it. It's only about fifteen minutes from there.

The neighborhood near the stadium isn't the nicest, but many neighborhoods near ballparks aren't. This neighborhood had a youngster who became the world heavyweight champion. As a boy, Evander Holyfield sold Cokes at Braves' games, and today, he's a frequent visitor, sitting twenty rows behind home plate. Once at a World Series game in St. Louis, I saw then heavyweight champion Michael Spinks, rooting for the Cardinals. (I never saw Muhammad Ali or Mike Tyson at a game.)

When the Braves became trendy, the celebrities began finding their way there. Holyfield's pal, rapper Hammer, former President Jimmy Carter, and of course, Ted and Jane. When Ted Turner bought the Braves in the seventies, he was a frustrated yachtsman who drank a bit and owned a truly terrible UHF television station.

By now, he's a statesman, having invented CNN, and turned that UHF station into the TBS network, and owns several other networks, too. In the seventies, he bought the Braves and the Hawks to help program his station, and found the time to manage the Braves for one game during a long losing streak in 1977. He lost, but like

Eddie Gaedel, he's in the record book. The commissioner at the time, Bowie Kuhn, prohibited Turner, or any future owner from managing a club, and Ted had to be satisfied with making billions. (Turner wasn't the first owner to manage a club, remember Connie Mack?)

As Turner became more occupied with his communications empire, he became less interested in baseball. Where he once was a regular at Braves games, by the nineties, he was rarely seen. When Ted met Ms. Jane, she was reportedly enamored with the fact that he owned a major league baseball team, and they began coming to games. Yes, Ted did appear to fall asleep on Jane's shoulder one night, and yes, they did get stuck in an elevator once after he was warned that if he insisted on getting on this hoary elevator, that it might be overloaded. The next day, I saw Ted and Jane get on that same elevator, and hustled aboard to see if history might repeat itself. Jane told Ted that he hadn't looked uptight when the elevator came to a rest for some forty-five minutes. Ted informed the rest of the passengers that he may have not looked uptight, but he was uptight.

During the 1991 season, Braves fans adopted "The Tomahawk Chop," and the organist led them in their moans. Other than large crowds, and this incessant moaning, there's really not much to recommend this ballpark. The seats are orange and blue and red and far away from the action, and the people are friendly. When your team is as good as the Braves, you ought to be friendly.

Atlanta will host the 1996 Olympics, and a new stadium will

be built for the Games adjacent to the current home of the Braves. After the Games conclude, tens of thousands of temporary seats will be removed from the outfield of the new park, and voila, a perfect new ballpark for the Braves will appear, just in time for the 1997 season. Before a game, Braves general manager John Schuerholz took my notebook and drew a sketch of what the new park would look like for the dubious reporter, sort of like Camden Yards with thirty or forty thousands temporary outfield seats.

It's not worth a visit to Atlanta to see Fulton County Stadium, but if the Braves and their magnificent pitching come to your town, they should be seen.

Chapter 11:

Taking the Hall in Vain

They all talk about it, but few understand. Vince Coleman, the brash Mets outfielder complained that playing in Shea Stadium could conceivably keep him out of the Hall of Fame. He didn't understand that just because as a young man he led the league in stolen bases, he wouldn't automatically deserve enshrinment in Cooperstown. He also wasn't, to be kind, realistic about his talent.

Milt Pappas, a fine pitcher in the sixties and early seventies thought he should get in, too. He received just a handful of votes, despite having better statistics than a contemporary who did gain entrance, Don Drysdale.

Reggie Jackson pined to be in the Hall of Fame, and would tell anyone who cared to listen that he deserved enshrinment. When he was a part-time coach for the Oakland A's, he kidded Rickey Henderson before a game that Rickey wouldn't make it to Cooperstown because he hadn't hit enough home runs. If he knew he had to hit home runs to be a Hall of Famer, Henderson would have become a long ball hitter instead of a base stealer, he answered. Jackson was an obvious choice when he was elected in 1993, and one of the great parts of any baseball season is the summer weekend when the new members of the Hall cry.

They don't mean to, but they always do. They're into middle age when elected, some are even older, and a few don't live to see their enshrinment. I was lucky to see Tom Seaver elected, and when he talked about his mentor, Mets manager Gil Hodges, he began to tear up. When he talked about his late mother, he couldn't continue. Seaver was a youthful looking 47 when he made the Hall, Hodges was 47 when he died.

By middle age, many of us have lost our parents, if we're fortunate enough to have had them that long, and baseball players, normally not given to reflection have a hard time with emotion. Hal Newhouser, the wartime star pitcher for the Detroit Tigers, saluted his mother in the audience. She was 95, but still drove her own automobile, he told the crowd.

Jim Palmer and Joe Morgan were enshrined together in 1990. It had rained for two days, and the ceremony was forced inside to a high school auditorium in Cooperstown. Perhaps six hundred were fortunate enough to be allowed inside the auditorium. Palmer, always one of the most polished of interviews, had difficulty finishing, but Morgan seemed up his election well. "We are very lucky," he concluded. We as fans were lucky to see these players perform, and we're lucky to have such a fitting showplace as the Hall of Fame.

Few active ballplayers ever visit it, the Hall's curator, Ted Spencer told me. During baseball's off season, it's cold in upstate New York, and not many players live in the area. One, Mark Lemke, of the Atlanta Braves, had been past the Hall a number of times, but didn't set foot inside until he brought a bat by after his spectacular 1991 World Series.

The Hall is remote, but these are baseball players we're talking about. They're used to having things done for them. They're used to room service, and not having to worry about lost luggage or missed plane connections. Few read books. I was amazed once to walk into the Toronto Blue Jays locker room and espy John Olerud buried in a Tom Clancy book, hard cover no less. Harold Reynolds, now of the Orioles, would visit the Smithsonian and the White House when he played for the Mariners on his trips to Baltimore. But, those men are seemingly few and far between.

When Greg Maddux was being courted by the Yankees after the 1992 season, General Manager Gene Michael took Maddux and his wife to a Broadway show, "Miss Saigon." Maddux, apparently hadn't seen a show during his many trips to New York in six years with the Cubs. His agent explained that upon his arrival in New York, he would order a room service cheeseburger and play Nintendo. I don't happen to play Nintendo, and I have ordered a room service cheeseburger on occasion, but wouldn't you think that maybe once, he would have explored New York. I could understand not going to the theater, I guess, but I would think that some players would be curious enough to venture out to a Broadway show. Maddux played six years in Chicago, and they have plenty of theaters and museums, and other cultural attractions there, but I guess he's happier now in Atlanta.

Look in any team's media guide. When you read player profiles, you'll find the most popular off field activities to be hunting, fishing, golf, movies and music. Once, I saw a player's biography, Jim Gott, then of the San Francisco Giants', list his hobby as opera. I was a bit skeptical, to say the least.

Occasionally, a player may go to Europe after the season, but more likely, they'll go on a hunting trip. I don't know if there's much hunting in Cooperstown.

I shouldn't be this hard on ballplayers, and their lack of culture. Few Americans have any, including this writer. Whenever I read a sports column in The New York Times by George Vecsey, I hold my breath and hope there will be no mentions of the great Afghanistan restaurants he has found in Minneapolis or St. Louis, while on a story, to prove that these cities are worthy.

I was once scoffed at when I asked if ballplayers vote--and that was by a writer.

Writers often scoff themselves at the self-centered behavior of players, when they discover that Vince Coleman, who will not make the Hall of Fame, had no idea who Jackie Robinson was. How could he not know his baseball history? Many of the writers, including me, weren't good enough to play baseball for very long, and we spent our time reading baseball books, while the players spent their time learning their craft. Not all players suffer from a lack of history. Reggie Jackson and Pete Rose are two who have a great sense of baseball history, but not only players suffer from historical amnesia. Most Americans do, too.

Americans know little of their own history. Ask a teenager who Adlai Stevenson was. See if they know that George Wallace, as a third party candidate in the presidential election of 1968, actually won some states, unlike Ross Perot. It's amazing that these kids would actually care about visiting a Hall of Fame. But,

103

some of them do. As we shall see shortly, some of them have other, more contemporary reasons for making the trek to Cooperstown.

To paraphrase Perot's soon to be forgotten running mate, Admiral James Stockdale, where is this Hall of Fame, and why is it there? It's in Cooperstown, New York, about 70 miles west of Albany, and not accessible off any main road. If you've been to Cooperstown, it's probably not by accident. Supposedly, baseball was invented by General Abner Doubleday in Cooperstown in 1839, though many a historian has cast aspersions on this story. More likely, baseball was taken from the British game of rounders, or even from cricket. Doubleday, as sportscaster Bill Stern told it in the forties, was summoned by President Abraham Lincoln's death bed, where Lincoln implored him: "Don't Let Baseball Die!"

Cooperstown is a charming small town. There are aren't any billboards, no McDonald's, no 7-11s. It's a one industry town, and that's baseball. Main Street is several blocks long, and there are restaurants and a Woolworth's and countless baseball memorabilia stores, and a realtor, showing houses that sell for several hundred thousand dollars, and a baseball museum.

No flashing lights tell you that the Hall of Fame is here, and if you don't look quickly, you'll miss it. It's a simple brick building, and it's a wonderful museum. There are few video exhibits, which to me is a blessing, when one thinks about all the times you've seen Carlton Fisk wave his home run fair. You've never even see a photograph of Babe Ruth allegedly calling his shot. When one sees a video played endlessly, it loses its meaning. You must leave something to the imagination. Harry Coyle, the best director of baseball on television in history, says that the only reason his camera operator recorded Fisk waving his home run fair was because a rat was discovered in the left field scoreboard in Fenway Park. The poor guy was frightened and changed his position, and was able to record that wonderful shot that Dick Stockton called.

I was in the stands for the sixth game of the 1977 World Series and saw Reggie Jackson hit his three home runs. I've seen the tape of his third home run so often that my recollection of the event is colored more by the tape than by my actual presence. I remember reading Norman Mailer talking about the phenomenon of Americans taking photographs at the Smithsonian. Americans didn't believe that something happened to them unless they had a photograph to cue them; they wouldn't trust their memory. I don't take photographs often. It's more fun to recollect on your own.

This Hall of Fame is much more a museum of the game than a Hall of Fame. They have wonderful old gloves and catcher's masks, and uniforms. You've figured out that I love uniforms, and they have exhibits on women in baseball and Negro League baseball, and all sorts of sheet music of long forgotten songs on the game. Don't you remember, "You're Going to Win that Ball Game--Uncle Sam!?"

The lack of video equipment is intentional, according to Mr. Spencer. He told me that he thought it wasn't special enough to have someone come hundreds of miles to visit a museum and see what they had seen on television last week. It's interesting to see children of the MTV generation take hours to painstakingly examine each exhibit. Perhaps, they'll visit a museum closer to where they live, and have a greater appreciation for artifacts.

More likely, they'll remember the seamier side of Cooperstown. The seamier side of a big city features crack, AIDS, prostitution, abject poverty. The seamy side of Cooperstown is the plethora of baseball card shops. It's been a recent phenomenon. You could spend thousands of dollars on a bat signed by a number of Hall of Famers at a store just a few feet from the Hall. Uniforms, balls, cards, photographs, they're all for sale. You can't walk down the street without hearing a carney barker beg for you to come inside his store to get autographs from Early Wynn or Monte Irvin or Ralph Kiner. I was flabbergasted at the several hundred people who would patiently queue up to pay $15, $30 or more for one of these guys to mechanically sign his name on a baseball card or ball. Some charged higher prices for signing bats. You aren't even allowed to hand the ball to the Hall of Famer yourself. You hand the ball to a supplicant, he hands it to the player, he signs it, returns it to the attendant, who hands it back to you. Players often don't converse, and occasionally don't even look up. This is serious business for them. Many make more money from signing autographs at card shows than they made in their entire baseball careers.

Many of the fans think of themselves as investors, hearing of the great sums of money to be made from collecting autographs and baseball cards. Unfortunately, for them, they don't personally know anyone who's ever made large amounts of money from collecting baseball memorabilia, unless it's the people who operate the stores. They read <u>Beckett's</u> magazine, <u>The Wall Street Journal</u> of card collecting, and try and ascertain whether their cards have risen in value from month to month.

A realist I am, and whenever a friend of mine, a well respected money manager and devoted fan, pines for the old days, and bemoans the era of free agency, I remind him that not long ago, when his contract expired, and he was a free agent, he sought the best deal for himself, too. But, I find this obsession of the Michael Milken wannabes a little difficult to take. The card market is hardly as liquid as the stock, bond or commodity markets. Whenever people moan that if only their mother hadn't tossed out their baseball cards twenty or thirty years ago, they could be rich, too, they're missing a salient point. It's only because millions of mothers tossed out card collections in shoeboxes, and many kids used their cards in their bicycle spokes that a Pete Rose rookie card is worth several hundred dollars. Lack of supply doesn't necessarily make a stock more expensive, rather it can inhibit a market in it. Lack of supply created the baseball card market, and now, with many more people buying cards, only one thing is guaranteed: None will make much money off the investment. My loving mother-in-law buys us a Franklin Mint proof set each Christmas, along with millions of others. Baseball cards in mint condition, twenty years from now, won't be worth much more than the proof sets. If the parents who are buying these sets of baseball cards become disgusted in 2013 that they haven't increased in value, and en masse, they're sent off to the recycling plant, perhaps by 2023, they'll increase in value once more, and a new card collecting craze can begin anew. First, there was tulip mania in Holland, then there was gold mania in 1980, and then, there was baseball card mania in Cooperstown.

Another friend of mine, the inspiration for this book, Mike Klein, has two houses. One in which he lives, and the other for his baseball memorabilia. This hematological oncologist, doesn't collect baseball cards, but collects books, magazines, programs, photos, and bats.

Each year, he attends the annual Hall of Fame induction weekend. Each year, the morning before the induction, he arises early to secure a place in line to purchase, at $100, plus New York State sales tax, a bat, autographed by the Hall of Famers. Just 500 bats are sold, and Klein will often invite those who share the bed and breakfast he rents each year to come along with him. If you buy a pair of bats, and sell them several hours later, you'll be able to pay for your weekend, he promises. He doesn't sell them, but he arose one year at 3 A.M. to camp out in the rain to be among the first to purchase these bats.

After he made his pilgrimmage to the Hall of Fame to buy the bats, he decided that perhaps three was a little early to get there. It would be safe to arrive at five or even six, he surmised, after all, "The supply is limited, and the demand is infinite," he promises. "Go to the streets of Calcutta, and see what the demand is for Hall of Fame bats," I challenge. He laughs, and backs off. Maybe that's why we've been friends for this long.

I promised in the introduction of this book not to talk about rotisserie or fantasy leagues. That was in the dead of winter, and now, the exhibition games have begun, and the book stores are full of these books, which promise you the most accurate projections of player performance.

In a fantasy league, each team manager is given an equal set amount of money to draft a roster. Aha, the insidious salary cap comes to baseball. Each player's value is published, and the team whose batters perform the best offensively, and whose pitchers

107

pitch most effectively, win. Fielding and intangibles matter not, and "rotisserie geeks," as they're known, don't root for team play, they just scoop up late editions of newspapers looking for West Coast box scores to see if their third baseman went 2 for 4.

It should be a harmless pastime, but I think it teaches its devotees that the individual matters more than the team, and not to pay attention to such insignificant details as hitting behind the runner, sacrificing properly or throwing to the right base.

Yes, you can be a wonderful fantasy league general manager if you know statistics, but as I have learned in my day job, fundamental analysis of the stock market and individual companies is much more effective than technical analysis, the studying of charts, in making money consistently. No one in a rotisserie league could go to a Babe Ruth league game and advise a major league team who to draft, so let's stop pretending.

While fantasy leagues may hurt the game intrinsically, they have created a veritable cottage industry in books, and helped the circulation of some newspapers, it's not a threat to the game itself, or the game's shrine. If you've never been to Cooperstown, you should make it a point to visit, but you don't have to hurry. It will be just as wonderful five or ten years from now, when the bottom falls out of the baseball card market, and when rotisserie leagues have long been forgotten.

Chapter 12:

Cleveland and Detroit: Only the Lonely

Just after I graduated from college in 1977, I set out on a trip by myself. I had majored in "Communication Arts and Sciences" at Queens College, and I thought the best way to get a job in television would be to start out in some smaller cities. I lived at home when I went to college, taking the subway and bus, ninety minutes each way, every day, for four years. I read voluminously on the train, and never tired of the trip.

My post graduate journey, was the first time I had been away from home by myself. It was the first of thousands of nights I would spend by myself in hotels. I didn't have the money for vacations between school years, I was busy going to summer school, or doing menial jobs for some spending money, and I didn't own a car. I took the train to Altoona, Pennsylvania, the bus to Johnstown, and another bus to Youngstown, Ohio. Those would be fine places to start my career, I thought. They're not that far from New York, and they were small enough so that they might give me a chance. After a week of pestering news directors and station managers to give this kid a break, I returned home without a job.

I took a final bus ride from Youngstown to Cleveland, and then took my initial airplane flight, back to New York. Before I flew back, I had to spend a night in Cleveland since no seats remained on the flight I wanted. I recall paying for my flight in cash, about $58, if memory serves me, and after I secured a ticket for the following day, I found a nearby hotel room, and decided to go to the ball park. What a novel idea.

This was 1977, the Indians weren't a national joke, but in the words of the newly elected president at the time, they certainly weren't a national treasure, either. Cleveland was about eighteen months away from hitting rock bottom, declaring bankruptcy, and while the Tribe wasn't a joke, the city was the subject of more than a few.

The Cuyahoga River caught fire in the sixties, and the one

time mayor, Ralph Perk, said he couldn't attend a reception honoring his party's president, Richard Nixon, because it conflicted with his bowling night. They dubbed the city, "The Mistake on the Lake," and its ballpark, then known as Cleveland Municipal Stadium, a few blocks from Lake Erie, wasn't looked upon favorably. In 1974, it was the scene of a rare forfeit, when fans stormed the field, fortified by having attended "Ten Cent Beer Night." God, it was a different time.

Ballpark gypsies, like me, were rare in the seventies, or at least, unpublicized. I had seen this place on television countless times, and it didn't look terribly attractive, but it was a ballpark, and I was away from home. I thought, what a terribly adventurous thing to do, spend a Friday night in Cleveland seeing a ball game.

I was impressed by Cleveland's Hopkins Airport. The subway was just below the main terminal, and the hotel was a short distance away. I took the subway downtown, and on the train, someone had two extra box seats, and he sold one to a fellow passenger, and the other to me. They turned out to be seats just two rows from the field, by the Indians' dugout, truly outstanding seats, but as most fans know, it's not been terribly difficult these past few decades to obtain good seats for an Indians game.

Peter Schmuck, late in the 1991 season, described a tiny crowd for a meaningless Indians-Orioles game as "having poured into Cleveland Stadium by the dozens." The crowd that night, I recall, wasn't abnormally small. It was somewhere in the low five figures, about average for the '77 Tribe.

The subway station was a short walk from the ballpark, and I excitedly half-walked, half-trotted towards it. In front, there was an enormous "Chief Wahoo," with his teeth gleaming, attached to the park. Besides not knowing when to say when, it was before political correctness, and demonstrations over use of Native American images as mascots. Come to think of it, it was even before Native Americans.

I remember how huge the park was, seating nearly 80,000, and only coming close to selling out on Opening Day. A decent crowd, one of 20,000, looks small there. Though the Cleveland Browns, and their rowdy fans, will continue to use what's know just called "Cleveland Stadium" as their home field, the Tribe will soon be moving.

It took years for the city to allow a new stadium to be built. It's the Gateway complex, and there will be an arena so that the Cavaliers can return downtown from suburban Richfield, too. The new Gateway Park, looks similar to Camden Yards, and lord, those long-suffering fans deserve it.

During my first visit, in an uncompetitive game, won by the Kansas City Royals, 12-2, I recall Indians designated hitter Rico Carty, on deck, just a few feet from my seat, continually smiling and gesturing to the fans. I wondered how he could he be so happy. After all, the Indians weren't a good club, they were getting pounded that night, and they were playing before small crowds in a cavernous ballpark. Now that I'm older, and Carty, who was a fine hitter in his time, is long out of the game, I know why he was so happy. He realized that he was playing major league baseball, and that no time in his life would ever be better, even if he was playing in Cleveland.

I vividly remember an older fan, who I'm afraid is probably no longer with us, admonishing Indian pitcher Rick Waits. "Take your time, Waits, take your time," he'd yell over and over. It didn't matter. Waits and the Tribe were going to lose, and this man with long, unkempt white hair, an unruly white beard, suspenders and a gray cap, had probably said this to countless hurlers over the years. He'd stand and holler, but he wasn't loud, he was plaintive, and I'm sorry he'll not be around to see the Tribe competitive once more.

John Adams and Mike Gesker will be around, though. Adams is the lonely fan who sits off in the bleachers, seemingly in another time zone, and beats his tom-tom, to encourage the Tribe. He's been there through thin and thin, and as the team improves, perhaps he won't be as lonely.

Gesker is a long-time friend of mine, who has lived in Baltimore his whole life, and paid his first visit to Cleveland Stadium in 1992. I worked with him for more than a decade, and then his job as a television writer was eliminated in late 1991, and he's struggled ever since. In his mid-forties, bald and bespectacled, with a cynically dry sense of humor, he works in a baseball card store at $5.50 an hour to supplement his state pension while he searches for full-time work. Occasionally, he'll manage to get an article published somewhere, but mostly he talks about "The Tribe, baby."

He grew up a Yankee, Packer and Celtic fan, admiring athletic excellence, but disdaining the hometown Orioles, Colts and Bullets. Disillusionment with Steinbrenner's Yankees led him to follow the Indians because as a youngster, he admired the exploits of Herb Score, Rocky Colavito and Jimmy Piersall, and as an adult, he identifies with the disenfranchised. That's a polite way of saying he is one with life's losers, but if you know this man, you know that's how he pictures himself.

He was briefly married in the eighties. On his wedding day, he wore a Yankee jersey underneath his suit, but I'm sure if he marries once more he'll wear an Indian blouse. It's about an eight hour drive from Baltimore to Cleveland, but Mike and his girlfriend made the trek anyway. It was like going to mecca for him; he was slightly troubled, he admitted, that after dating this woman for an extended period of time, their initial overnight trip was to Cleveland, but like Mount Everest, it was there.

In a small apartment full of several thousand books, magazines, newspapers and baseball memorabilia, he lives quietly with several cats, waiting for phone to ring, and patiently waiting for the Tribe to win. While other teams who haven't won a championship in some years play in media centers such as Chicago and Boston, Cleveland is hardly heard from, except as a joke. The Cubs and the Red Sox may have contending teams, but Cleveland hasn't seen a pennant race since the Eisenhower presidency. If Gesker lived in Cleveland, he'd probably be a Tiger fan, but he doesn't, and when the throngs begin to pack the new Gateway park for the improved and exciting Indians, I think he'll have to find a new team to identify with, perhaps the Washington Generals.

About 170 miles west of Cleveland lies America's most maligned city. It's Detroit, and unlike Cleveland, which pulled through the eighties quite nicely, and even has a Ritz Carlton not far from the ballpark, Detroit is one of America's most contentious cities.

With a large black majority, and a mayor who seems intent on prolonging his reign rather than actually helping any of his impoverished citizens, Detroit is home to historic Tiger Stadium, on the edge of downtown.

For years, I had looked forward to visiting Tiger Stadium, but it wasn't until 1989, several years after marrying Susan, that I visited. Her parents lived in a suburb, about thirty-five minutes from the ballpark, and as a lifelong resident and connossieur of big cities, I couldn't wait to see Detroit. I had heard all sorts of awful things about it, but I kept reading that Tiger Stadium was another one of baseball's jewels, along with Wrigley and Fenway. After having visited Detroit several times, and been to Tiger Stadium, I have to admit I was partially wrong. Detroit is a horrible place, and I don't think Tiger Stadium is much better.

I truly wanted to like it, but I couldn't. Tiger Stadium was a throwback. Drive your car, park it on one of the many nearby lots, and walk to the ballpark. The neighborhood is dank and depressing, with a few neighborhood taverns, complete with booths with drab brown imitation leather that sticks to your clothes after a few minutes. The decor and waitresses haven't changed since the fifties, and they have jukeboxes blaring such old standards as "Mona Lisa." Holdouts against the passage of time, these establishments are, back when people actually used the terms "tavern" or "saloon."

No, there shouldn't be Bennigan's or Houlihan's across the street from every ballpark, and every stadium shouldn't be indistinguishable, but there ought to be other places for a family to have a bite to eat before stepping into the ballpark.

I understand that new owner Mike Ilitch has vowed to upgrade the concessions at Tiger Stadium, and it's a good thing. There wasn't much there, except for Domino's pizza, which made sense. Former owner Thomas Monaghan, founded Domino's. Illitch was the founder of the arch-rival, Little Caesar's, and hockey fans tell me has done an outstanding job at promoting the Detroit Red Wings, who play in Joe Louis Arena, a short distance away, downtown.

In-town stadiums are much better than suburban pleasure palaces, but if you're going to have an in-town stadium, there ought to be some place else to go before or after the game. The streets are eerily deserted a short time after the game. No one goes to downtown Detroit, even at five o'clock on a Sunday afternoon. I have been in almost every city of size in North America, and never have I seen such a desolate downtown as in Detroit.

There aren't any major stores, but Greektown is next to downtown, and if you like Souvlaki, there's no better place to find it. The Renaissance Center, is close by, but it's been a colossal economic failure. The Ritz Carlton isn't near the park as it is in Cleveland, but in suburban Dearborn. Most visiting teams stay in Dearborn, a good half hour drive, choosing to disdain the nearby downtown Omni.

The ballpark neatly fits on the streets, but it's painted a dingy shade of green, and the employees all look as if they've worked there since the Harding administration. With the concessions unimaginative, and nothing to do in the surrounding area for children who may be marginal fans at best, it's no wonder that attendance has fallen sharply in recent years.

Only true baseball fans make it to Tiger Stadium. If you have a good seat, there aren't many better places to watch a game, but on our first visit, I took my young niece and nephew on an exploration mission, and found there really weren't many good seats. There are probably more seats in fair territory here, on a percentage basis, than in any other stadium, other than Arlington.

114

Many of these seats are tremendously far from the action, perhaps five hundred feet away. The seats by the field are intimate; you do feel a part of the game, and if you're fortunate enough to be Ernie Harwell, the radio and television broadcast locations are closer than any other in the big leagues. Balls come back so quickly that Ernie brings a net to catch them. The writing press sits in a rooftop box behind plexiglass. The stands are low enough so that balls often bounce against the glass.

The Tigers promotion philosophy for years has apparently been, open up the gates, and they'll come. With the Detroit area economy a fragile one, and lots of other outdoor activities on summer weekends in Northern Michigan, baseball hasn't been as popular in Detroit as it ought to be.

Illich has promised more aggressive promotions, and a food court, like those found in many other ballparks. Will this be enough to save Tiger Stadium? Does Tiger Stadium deserve being saved?

The new owner says he'll reserve judgment on whether or not a new park is necessary. He says he'll try and spruce up the park. He's done well with the Red Wings, and the downtown Fisher Theatre, so we must wish him well. The old regime said a new park was necessary for the Tigers to survive, and if a new one wasn't built in a location closer to the suburbs, the team would consider moving out of town as the Lions and Pistons have. Mayor Young wanted a new park built close to downtown, and champions of keeping the Tigers on the corner of Michigan and Trumbull have been vocal in their opposition to a new ballpark. Attend any game there, and you'll undoubtedly see signs, or receive a leaflet imploring Michiganders to oppose the relocation of the Tigers. "If they build it, we won't come," was a favorite one.

It's only the real fans who haven't given up on the Tig-uhs, and now, for the first time, a few new faces are being spotted at the ballpark. Though the city and the neighborhoods surrounding the ballpark are overwhelmingly black, not many African-American fans have made their way into Tiger Stadium. But, with the emergence of Cecil Fielder as a superstar, more and more minority fans have started going to the games, long-time observers report.

As a youngster growing up in New York, I was old enough to remember the "old" Madison Square Garden, about a mile north of the present one. Oldtimers would talk about the marquee. It was a favorite meeting place for your friend, brother-in-law, date or bookmaker, by Nedick's, where you'd grab a hot dog and Orange Julius before a game. On the Garden's marquee, would read: Tonight: NBA Doubleheader: Cincinnati vs. St. Louis Knicks vs. Philadelphia 1st game 6:30. They have a marquee in Tiger Stadium, too, and like the old one at Madison Square Garden, it's not electronic. Today: Milw 1:35, it reads, with the worn black letters spelling out the remaining games of the homestand on Michigan Avenue, near the main entrance.

I've been hard on Tiger Stadium, and Detroit, but it too, like the other parks, should be seen. It's not as charming as Wrigley or Fenway, but it is, in its way, a throwback, to baseball of years gone by. With only real fans attending, and not many amenities, you'll appreciate once again, the newer parks, and you'll be a part of something that once was in baseball, and will never be again. You should experience it because once gone, we'll truly never see the likes of Tiger Stadium again.

Chapter 13:

Domes, Sweet Domes

The unholy trinity of baseball is the designated hitter, artificial turf, and the domed stadium. Undoubtedly, expanded playoffs will soon take their place in the traditionalist's hall of shame.

While the d.h. may have its share of defenders, artificial turf and the domes have few. I've come not to bury domes, nor to raze them, but to explain them.

I've viewed perhaps a dozen games under domes, so I can't qualify as an indoor baseball maven, but if I lived in Houston, I'd be just as enthusiastic about the game as I am now. It's just different.

When the Astrodome opened in 1965, Texas was booming. Their own Lyndon Johnson was the President then, and he had recently been reelected by one of the largest margins in history. Vietnam hadn't begun to sap his popularity, and ours was to be "The Great Society." Houstonians referred to the Astrodome, as "The Eighth Wonder of the World." Judge Roy Hofheinz, a friend of LBJ's, and the owner of the Astros, had lobbied successfully for the construction of the dome, saying the heat, humidity and mosquitos of Houston in the summer made outdoor baseball miserable.

The Houston franchise began life as the Colt 45s when they began play in 1962. For three seasons, they played at ramshackle Colt Stadium, and to avoid the heat, the National League allowed the team to play the major's first Sunday night games.

When the Astros moved to the Dome, it was quickly discovered that glare would be a problem, and the roof was ordered painted. That task completed, it was found that grass wouldn't grow without sunlight. Thus, the birth of artificial turf, and a generation of carpers was given new material. Having attended my first baseball game less than eighteen months before the Astrodome premiered, I was unaware that there was much, if any whining about baseball before domes. What did the traditionalists moan about before artificial turf, domes and the designated hitter?

Washington has its Beltway mentality. Houston has its 610 loop. While the Washington Beltway encircles the city, never coming closer than several miles to the District of Columbia, the 610 loop is at many points, within the city of Houston. The Astrodome is located off the South loop, not far from the West loop. Got that straight? There's no neighborhood nearby. Signs direct game day traffic to the exits marked "domed stadium," and nearby, there are the usual suspects: chain hotels, Bennigan's, and across the freeway, an amusement park.

It doesn't look imposing from the highway. It's funny when you look at it to think that this was what all the fuss was about. It's now just one of the pre-Teflon domes. Look at the Superdome in New Orleans, a pre-Teflon dome. Now, that looks imposing. It's much larger than the Astrodome, seating perhaps fifteen thousand more, and much more of a Convention Hall. The Teflon domes are less offensive to look at, both for the spectator, and those who live or work nearby, and have to see them regularly.

Inside, the Astrodome can be kind of depressing. It's not intimate, it's nondescript. Of all the ballparks I've been to, I can find the fewest words to describe the experience of attending a game there. Football is much more popular in Texas than baseball ever has been; there's not the baseball tradition that the East, Midwest and California have. Before major league baseball ever migrated west, the Pacific Coast League's brand of baseball was the best in the minor leagues', and drew respectable crowds. The gatherings were much larger than in the Texas League, where the brand of baseball played wasn't nearly as high. The PCL season, because of the favorable West Coast weather was even longer than in the big leagues, and while Californians had no first hand knowledge of the majors, they knew more about baseball than Texans did.

Texans attended Astros games in huge numbers in the early years of the Dome, when it was a novelty, and during the two seasons, 1980 and 1986, that the Astros won their division. The Astrodome is considered baseball's most difficult home run park.

Randy Bass, who has had two terms of duty with the Astros claims that the ball travels further in the Dome when its full, and in recent years, it hasn't been full often.

The past winter has been the snowiest in the Northeast in several years, and just three weeks from Opening Day, the worst March storm in memory dumped a foot of snow in the east. That storm made me think of domes. If a blizzard struck Minneapolis on Opening Day, it wouldn't matter to the fans there, and while I love being outdoors during the season, baseball inside is better than no baseball at all.

After the Astrodome came the Kingdome. While it was thought that Houstonians wouldn't attend games in the summer due to heat and bugs, Washingtonians wouldn't flock to baseball games in the rain, either. After the Pilots' disasterous season in Seattle, it was decided that the only way a team could survive in the Pacific Northwest would be to play in a domed stadium.

It doesn't often rain heavily in Seattle during the season, but it drizzles regularly, and rain and baseball don't mix. A problem with baseball in Seattle is that unlike many other cities, there are countless alternative activities to the game on a summer Sunday, particularly when the weather is nice.

Seattle is depressing when it rains. It is perhaps the most spectacular city in America when it's sunny. There isn't humidity, the air is clear, and the temperature is in the seventies. Boating, fishing and hiking at nearby Mount Rainer can be stiff competition, particularly when you realize the Mariners have yet to be a contender, and have recorded just one winning season.

Many people make the mistake of thinking that such an outstanding city should have an equally outstanding ballpark. It's not great, but I like it better than the Astrodome. Located just on the edge of downtown, the Kingdome is better known for being the home of the Seattle Seahawks, and their boisterous fans. The Mariner crowds have been sparse, and not enthusiastic. The stadium seems more intimate than does the Astrodome, and much more intimate than Montreal's Olympic Stadium. The ball seems to carry well, and

119

in recent years, management has tried to spruce up the park by constructing an old-time scoreboard in right field with scores of all major league games. The Kingdome was the first dome I saw a game in, in 1984, and I was struck by the novelty. The crack of the bat seemed louder. Perhaps it was because of the small crowd. The outfield fences seemed much closer indoors. At an open-air major league park, hitting a home run, even in batting practice, would be a fool's fantasy, even for a reasonably in-shape adult such as myself. At the Kingdome, a home run suddenly seemed attainable, though in reality, the fences were no closer than they were, in say, Baltimore. I think I'll reserve my batting practice for an occasional visit to a pitching machine.

I'm not sure what the best ballpark in the majors is. It could be Wrigley Field, it could be Camden Yards, maybe it's Fenway Park. But, I am sure what the worst ballpark in the majors is: Montreal's Olympic Stadium.

Built for the 1976 Olympics, the Expos moved from funky Jarry Park in 1977. Phillies broadcaster Andy Musser told me that it was more like an intimate recreational league park than a major league stadium. It sat around 30,000 fans, and in the first few years of major league baseball in Montreal, the fans loved it. Gene Mauch managed the team in those days, and in 1973, he had the fifth year Expos in contention in a year when the Mets won the division with a record just three games over .500.

When the team moved to Olympic Stadium, Dick Williams was its manager, and they were authentic contenders, and of course, the crowds were large. Several years into their occupancy, the province of Quebec fulfilled a long promised goal, to make this stadium the first retractable dome.

The cost overruns for the stadium and the Olympics were mind-boggling, beware Atlanta, and it was quickly discovered that the retractable roof was hard to work. The stadium was owned by the province of Quebec, and in the best tradition of "good enough for government work," it was decided that paying overtime for a maintenance worker to operate the dome was against the rules. Thus, for night and weekend games, it would have to be decided in advance whether the dome would be open or closed.

I haven't seen this place open, but it's awful when it's closed. I've not visited since 1988, and they claim it's been slightly improved since then, and it sure could have used it. The roof was orange, and when combined with the glare from the lights, it was difficult to follow the ball. The seats were far from the field, and the atmosphere felt like a hospital.

The Montreal Metro has a station that lets you off right at the park, but inside, despite Youppi, the furry Orange Expo mascot, who insisted on saying hello to my friends, it's dead. No one keeps score, except of course for me. No one appreciates the subleties of the game. I don't appreciate the subleties of hockey, but it would be nice to hear some enthusiasm. From watching Expos games on television in the early days, I remember the hearty cheers for "Le Grande Orange," Rusty Staub. This most wonderful of all North American cities, with its outstanding restaurants, culture and attractive people, just doesn't get baseball.

As Dick Williams explained in his book, baseball players' reluctance to play in Montreal wasn't because the taxes were high, and that it was a foreign country. They just have a difficult time accepting an experience where they're not the center of importance, he believes. I would have thought that an odd player or two would have enjoyed playing in Montreal because of the culture, and the unique feeling of the town. Not. It isn't very far from Boston or New York, but it just isn't attractive to players. None live there year round, and few take the trouble to attempt to learn French. Staub, a native of New Orleans, made a concerted effort to learn the language, and the fans appreciated that.

It must be difficult for Latin players in Montreal. The Expos and Blue Jays have extensive scouting networks in Latin America, and have signed many fine Hispanic players. It's difficult enough to learn English as an adult, and many have done remarkably well at that. How many Americans who play winter ball in Latin America have bothered to learn Spanish? After learning rudimentary English

121

in the minor leagues for several years, a Latin player lands in Montreal, where French is the first language of the majority of the population. He must feel lost. How many of you can communicate in two languages? How many can communicate in three?

If you've got to play indoors, I would prefer the Metrodome or SkyDome. The Metrodome's predecessor, Metropolitan Stadium, in suburban Bloomington, hosted its last game in 1981, and it was the last major league stadium that I failed to see a game in. Near the airport, it's now the site of "The Mall of America," the largest shopping area in the country.

Was it necessary to have a dome in Minneapolis? According to Steve Cannon, the long-time radio talk show host of WCCO, it was. Early in the season, it was so cold that bullpen tenants built fires to stay warm, he swears.

The Hubert H. Humphrey Metrodome is located on the outskirts of downtown Minneapolis, and on a nice day or night, you'll feel it's wasteful to play indoors, but during the 1991 World Series, when the temperatures outdoors were in the forties with heavy winds whipping, I was glad. In the press box in Minneapolis, the temperature both outdoors and indoors is announced.

It's a Teflon dome, and it reminds one of the hometown Pillsbury doughboy, all white and puffy. It's much more attractive than the aforementioned domes. There are lots of parking lots nearby, access and eggress is relatively simple, and it's not symmetrical.

The field boxes aren't close to the field, but the seats in the outfield are. The outfielders are protected from the fans by plexiglas, which can cause a glare, making it difficult at times to follow play. Besides the puffy white roof, which can also make following fly balls a chore, there's the modern day "Green Monster" in right field. The enormous dark blue, "Hefty Trash Bag" makes this dome unlike all others. Its dimensions are suspiciously like Camden Yards', and Jim Kaat, the Twins broadcaster says the short right field doesn't necessarily make home runs easier to come by, but it increases the number of doubles greatly.

122

The noise from a large crowd can be impressive, though I had heard so many stories about the roar during the 1987 World Series that I expected much worse. After all, I grew up listening to my mother attempt to talk over the roar of the IRT. That was much louder.

The Metrodome's master of ceremonies is Bob Casey, who has been the public address announcer as far back as I can remember. Casey loves to growl: "Centerfielder, number 34, Kirrrrbeee Puckk-ettt!," or grunt: "Designated Hitter, number 44, Chheeel-lee Davv-is." The crowd follows his enthusiam by waving those stupid homer hankies, better than throwing bottles, I guess. The loudness of the crowd, the public address system, the asymmetrical field and the Twins' fine play in recent years make this dome the dome I'd choose to call the least objectionable of all. It's hard to have a favorite dome, you understand, but if you pressed me...

SkyDome, now that's a strange one. My first games in Toronto were at Old Exhibition Stadium, which still stands, not far from SkyDome. It's on the grounds of the Canadian National Exhibition, home of the nationwide fair each August, and it was built for Canadian football, 110 yards long, 55 yards wide. It was the worst park for baseball I could imagine. On the shores of Lake Ontario, it would get a little nippy from time to time, and it had absolutely no atmosphere to go along with its irregular dimensions.

Many of the rows had forty seats or more. It wasn't much fun when someone wanted to get up during play. It wasn't any fun to sit near first base during a night game and watch the sun set in your eyes since the stadium was set up north-south instead of east-west. While fans would talk about Wrigley Field, Fenway Park, Tiger Stadium or Atlanta-Fulton County being the best home run parks in baseball, I would have nominated Exhibition. The balls seemed to fly out of that place.

When SkyDome opened in 1989, the Blue Jays had been a contender for some years, and fans expected quality baseball. They got that, but when they visited SkyDome, they also received a most unusual ballpark experience.

You've heard about the hotel that overlooks the field, where the couple made love in front of an entire stadium. You've read about the "Hard Rock Cafe," and the restaurant where fans can watch the game as well as eat an overpriced buffet. There's the large McDonald's, with the larger than normal prices. There are the cigarette machines which sell a pack for $7.00 Canadian. If that isn't incentive to quit, I don't know what is.

There's the quiet roof, which can open and close in a matter of minutes, and the bullpens, which can't be seen from the field of play. The dugouts select the bullpen video feed channel to monitor progress on television. There are also those awful statues out front of the stadium. Brass statues of players, managers, umpires, even a beer bellied, hot dog belching, sneering fan. I hope the people of Ontario didn't have to pay for that, too. The stadium suffered from cost overruns, what a surprise, but at least they sell out each night.

When I took my wife to a game, the dome was closed, and she complained that she was overstimulated. There was simply too much else happening for her to concentrate on the field. There was music playing, the huge scoreboards with their basic baseball information and elaborate commercials. My criticism is that with all this technology, I'd like to see some more interesting information on the board.

SkyDome is convenient. Located in downtown Toronto, easily accessible by bus and subway, it's a giant magnet with well behaved crowds. With excellent teams and this unusual playpen, the Blue Jays have regularly sold out in their years at SkyDome. When will the novelty wear off? Can it be Canada's version of Dodger Stadium, still terrific after all these years?

It's obviously an expensive proposition to attend games in a country that's not as rich as the United States. I jokingly asked a Canadian friend if there were second mortgages in Canada. He said his country even had third mortgages. They'll need them to regularly attend games at SkyDome.

In 1993, while on a business trip to Japan, I attended my first baseball game in Asia. It was in the Tokyo Dome, the first domed stadium in Japan. The Japanese liked the domes so much that they have now opened a second one, and plans have recently been announced for a third one.

The Tokyo Dome bears a striking resemblance inside to the Metrodome, seats in blue, with a press box close to the action at the end of the first deck. From the outside, it looks more like the classical concrete Astrodome-Superdome-Kingdome mold rather than the Hoosier-Metrodome-Silverdome collapsable roof. Outside, it's kind of garish. Inside, the baseball stinks.

By know, you know that I'll not leave a game voluntarily. In Tokyo, I left during the middle of the seventh inning. They don't have a seventh inning stretch there.

I saw a game between the Nippon Ham Fighters and the Danei Lions. In Japan, teams are not named after the city in which they play, but rather after the corporations that own them. The country's most popular team, the Yankees of Japan, are the Yomiuri Giants, who regularly sell out the Tokyo Dome. The Ham Fighters draw respectably in their games at "The Big Egg," but often don't sell out. If you watch for several innings, you may understand why.

Each of the twelve teams in Japan is allowed two gaijin or foreigners. There are two leagues, the Central and the Pacific. One allows the designated hitter, and one doesn't. The pitchers, rarely Americans, are small, and in baseball parlance, "pitch backwards," starting most hitters with breaking balls, and only rarely resort to fastballs.

In Tokyo Dome, at least, there were no bullpens on the field. Perhaps they were under the stands, but when pitching changes were made, the relief pitchers mysteriously appeared. A fence, perhaps a third the size of the backstop, kept balls from screaming into the stands for the entire length of foul territory. If a fan catches a ball, they politely return it to an usher.

Vendors are usually attractive women in brightly colored outfits, and they will pour a patron's beer from a bottle. And, the San Francisco Giants have nothing on their distant cousins in

Tokyo: All public address announcers in Japan are women.

Besides pitchers not challenging the hitters, the Japanese play a radical form of Gene Mauch baseball--"little ball" to the extreme, nearly always playing for one run, bunting, hitting behind runners, and hitting to the opposite field. The quality of play seems to be about on the AA level.

The foreigners, Americans, with a few Latins, are usually recognizable only to passionate fans. Mel Hall, Jesse Barfield and Lloyd Moseby were the usual, fading American players attempting to prolong their careers by making much more money than they would be able to at home. Cecil Fielder was a credible player in his early years, went to Japan, became a star, and returned to greater stardom. He was the true exception.

Japanese like to brag about their society featuring nearly "full employment." Watch a game there, and you'll understand why. There are six umpires for all games, two stationed in front of the outfield wall.

A choice of Japanese and western food is available. Hot dogs and hamburgers were sold, but I chose the bento, a fancy Japanese box lunch or dinner that features rice, meat, fish and sushi.

Fans of the opposing teams sat in the left and right field bleachers, cheering incessantly when their team was at bat. They seemed not to care about the action on the field. Cheerleaders with bugles, drums and noisemakers led the cheering and noisemaking while the rest of crowd sat watching impassionly.

They applauded home runs, but I didn't. A tacky American custom, the mascot, has found its way westward. Whenever a Ham Fighter would hit one out, the Ham would greet him at home plate, hand him a miniature Ham, and the player would toss it in the stands.

The seats were expensive. A box seat cost 48,000 yen, around $45 dollars, but bleacher seats could be had for around $4 dollars. With all the talk about Japanese goods being superior to American products, this good was clearly inferior, and I hope the Japanese don't dump their baseball here.

Chapter 14:
The Press Box: What It's Really Like

When I first contemplated writing this book several years ago, I thought it would be great fun if I approached this as a fan who was fortunate enough to gain access to baseball for a season, and got to ask questions of baseball people that a fan might want to know. I'd go to the different parks, and try and be both a fan and a writer.

Very quickly, I began looking upon myself as a writer instead of a fan, and that may have been a mistake. But, I did, in the course of writing this book, get to be a writer. I fill in when the regular reporter assigned to cover the Orioles from United Press International can't make it. I get paid $25 a game. I have a blast.

My job was to cover the game, and then phone in a story with six outs to go, updating as I went along. Occasionally, the desk would make special requests: Could I ask Nolan Ryan about his future? Could I get some special stuff on Brady Anderson? Initially, I didn't have my own laptop computer, so the work was slightly tedious. I quickly began good at dictating while concentrating on the final outs. I've now joined the laptop crowd.

When my friends found out what I was doing, they were envious. Imagine getting to watch ball games for free! Imagine getting to meet and talk to major league athletes! As the more sophisticated of you must realize, it's not all, as they say, it's cracked up to be.

I had no illusions about what major league ballplayers would be like. My expectations were low, having read many critical articles in recent years. The press has done a fine job in presenting athletes the way the are: some obnoxious, some nice, and the majority disinterested. I wasn't disappointed.

Most writers arrive several hours before a game. Major league clubhouses open three and-one-half hours before a game, and stay upon until forty-five minutes before the scheduled first pitch. After the game, they're opened ten minutes after the final out. A "beat" writer, who covers a major league team on a daily basis, often has to write not only a story about the game, but a story of notes on the team. For this notes column, he or she will talk to the manager and several players before game time. These notes are generally written before the game begins, allowing the writer to concentrate on the game.

The writer must do this for each game, and depending upon the length of the game, if they're writing for a morning paper, their story may include quotes from key participants. In these days of games lasting more than three hours, it may occasionally be difficult for a complete story to be written in time to make the deadline for the paper you may have delivered to your home.
During the post-season, with later starting times and longer games, often lasting past midnight, and inflexible deadlines, most readers get an incomplete story. Thus, the carping from writers, who call for day games in the World Series, or earlier start times.

Managers generally meet with the press before each game. Orioles manager John Oates, admittedly a favorite of mine, was generous with his time, and lacking in guile. His answers were straightforward, and he avoided cliches, when possible. He was never a glad-hander, and if a serious question was asked, he would answer seriously. He could be short upon occasion, but his directness and civility were most appreciated. I learned much baseball from him.

Tom Lasorda, whom Oates says he has learned much from about handling the media onslaught, was alternately charming and testy. If a reporter was baiting him, Lasorda often would take the bait and snarl at his interregator. I found that even when in a foul mood, a serious baseball question about strategy would elucidate a cogent and serious answer.

Once I felt lucky. For nearly an hour, he began talking about his upbringing, his goals, the loss of his young son, and his achievements. Funny, introspective and seemingly honest, the handful of us who were in his office were captivated. We went away raving about his performance, and our good fortune. I couldn't wait to get home to transcribe his thoughts. Several months later when I saw an interview he had given Mike Lupica for "Esquire," and saw the same routine verbatim, I could see how easy it was for even experienced Lasordoligists to be taken in.

Oates was honest, too. One night, alone in the visiting manager's office in Texas, he talked about his job. He had especially admired Dick Howser when he played for him. He made "me feel like the MVP on the 1980 New York Yankees, when I was the 26th man on a 25 man club. I was just there because they didn't have anybody else. I would sprint from the bullpen to catch a game whether we were behind thirteen to nothing, or winning thirteen to nothing just because of the way he treated me."

He tried to treat his fringe players honorably. In his first year, Dave Johnson, a pitcher who had spent years in the minor leagues before spending several seasons in the big leagues was openly insecure about his place with the Orioles. Johnson would talk about his anxieties. "The opportunity's here, and it's gone. Sometimes, it's hanging out there, and you go to reach for it, and it's gone. It can happen that fast. If I have a bad game, I think, am I going to pitch for the Orioles again? It's day to day, it's an emotional roller coaster. God, it's amazing."

Oates identified with players like Johnson, though he knew that he had to have more skilled pitchers than he on the team if it were to improve. "I spent fifteen years that way," he said of Johnson's jitters. "My biggest regreat of my playing days was that I didn't enjoy being a major league player. Every day I went through what Dave Johnson went through. It's out of his hands. It was out of my hands. What good did it do to never sleep, ten years in a row?"

"If I was good enough to keep a job, I kept it, if I wasn't all the begging, 'please, please Mr. (Jim, general manager of the Dodgers at the time) Campanis, I'm the best catcher you have, don't release me' wouldn't help. I spent ten years worrying about whether I was going to be released tomoorow. I should have enjoyed every day of ten years."

Oates would talk while his team was taking batting practice. We would surround him in a semi-circle, most times eight or ten, and while he talked to us, his eyes never left the field. He occasionally would kid me about my ability to write while looking at him, and not looking down. The players would rarely kid us. Glenn Davis would ask me for whom I was writing, and what was the progress on my book, but other than a "how ya' doin'?," the players didn't have much contact with the writers.

It wasn't much fun hanging around a clubhouse. I felt like an interloper. I didn't belong, and early in my project, I had difficulty telling players without their uniform. Most teams have practice jerseys they wear for batting and fielding practice without their names, and I learned quickly to carry a scoresheet with me so that I might recognize them by their numbers.

Some would sit in front of their lockers and read their fan mail. They would autograph their baseball cards and talk without looking at you. Few showed any interest in the world outside of baseball. I didn't much enjoy this part.

Occasionally, I would find a player who was enjoyable to talk to. Nolan Ryan was always nice and polite, George Brett was, too. Jose Canseco could be nice, and I even caught Barry Bonds on some of his good days. Cal Ripken was cool and aloof, and that was perhaps my biggest surprise. I had seen Ripken's first game, on my 25th birthday in 1981. He was a pinchrunner, and scored the winning run. I saw him hit his first home run, on the following opening day, and saw his streak begin a few weeks later. I saw his brother's first game, too. He had always been portrayed as the All-American boy in Baltimore, and it came as somewhat of a shock to find that he often ducked the press after a game.

A favorite trick of his, and many other players was to hide in the trainer's room after a game. This room is off-limits to outsiders, and those who wished to avoid contact would stay there, and then head directly to the showers, hoping that most reporters wouldn't stay long.

Once before a game, I cornered Ripken by his locker where he was signing batting gloves, and I asked him if I might talk to him for a few minutes. He politely declined. When he did talk, he was a fine interview, introspective and intelligent. It seemed silly of him, I thought, to be so aloof. Once in Texas, after a game, a local reporter asked if he might have a minute. "Not really," he grumbled, but he allowed a few questions. In Texas, it wasn't as if he had anywhere to go. The hotel was just several hundred feet from the ballpark, and there was no bus to catch.

I've always admired his talent, as do most of the writers, but I found few who enjoyed dealing with him. His brother Bill, with whom he played for nearly six seasons, wasn't nearly as bright, but he was friendlier. His father, one-time manager and long-time coach, Cal Senior, was a downright grouch. He was the epitome of an old-time "baseball man." His answers, when he did talk, were full of cliches, and he was sure to use the word "baseball" in nearly every sentence. "In the game of baseball," he'd begin. Once he shocked me, though, by actually recognizing me, and saying hello. Cal Junior, never did.

After a game, when the press is allowed into the locker room, most head straight to the manager's office unless there was a compelling individual performance. Oates was nearly always even-tempered and patient, and he quickly learned how to provide sound bites for radio and television. The print reporters would allow the radio and television guys to ask their superficial questions before they might ask the more difficult ones. They might ask about his reasoning for a specific move he made, (always a favorite of mine) about a performance of a pitcher, how a batter was swinging, and did he contemplate making changes in the batting order.

Before a game, he would talk about the prognosis for injured players, and perhaps a controversy from the night before. Occasionally, he'd give us a baseball quiz. As a catcher in the big leagues for a decade, he had caught nearly all of the 200 game winners at the time of his retirement in 1981, and could we name them. I was proud that I came up with several of the names. Don Sutton, Luis Tiant, Jim Palmer, Steve Carlton, Gaylord Perry, and

Jim Kaat he caught. Tom Seaver and Ferguson Jenkins he hadn't.

After batting practice, we would go up to the press room and eat. We would often argue, and I learned a lot of baseball from the other writers here. The scouts would also congregate here, with a table of their own.

Some of the scouts were "advance" men, who were following the participating teams for the teams that would soon play them. Others were scouting a city or division for a team, looking for trades in the future. Others were sent to look at specific players by teams interested in trading for them. Lots of recognizable names remained in the game by scouting, former players, coaches and managers. They sit in each park, seven or eight rows behind home plate, some keeping score, some making notes, others just watching. Some would be happy to share information, others kept to themselves. During the 1992 season, scouts from the Colorado Rockies and Florida Marlins were often in evidence, and during the latter stages of a pennant race, scouts descend on contending teams parks' hoping to pick up useful information for the League Championship Series and World Series.

The writers usually kept to themselves, and so did the electronic types. As an electronic type most of the time, I found this dichotomy fascinating. At the ballpark, I tended to identify more with the writers, most of whom were incredibly generous with their time and information.

It was nice just being one of the guys, too. In my job as producer of "Wall Street Week With Louis Rukeyser," I am inundated with requests from public relations people who would like their clients to appear on the program. It's nice to be in such a position, where I only occasionally have to struggle for a noted guest, and where most people eagerly accept my invitation. I enjoyed seeing what it was like to have to grapple with several dozen others for a few minutes of a player's time after a game, and not be treated as special.

A common refrain of the guys in the press room was the disillusionment many felt after covering sports for a few years.

I never labored under illusions, and I thought it silly that anyone else did. To me, a ballplayer owes the public his best performance on the field. He should talk to the press, he should occasionally sign autographs, and should occasionally make an appearance on behalf of a charity or a youth baseball organization. It shouldn't surprise us that some of the players are womanizers, drinkers, drug abusers or louts. Some of the press, and some of the fans are, too.

It's the media's fault in many ways that the public has the wrong impression of athletes. We lionize them instead of leaving them alone. We shouldn't care about their off-field activities, unless they're having an impact on their performance on the field. I wish parents wouldn't give their children money to obtain a player's autograph at a card show. They're contributing to the false image of these players. We expect ballplayers to be extraordinary, but how would you like it, after you've played hard for three hours, and practiced for several hours beforehand, to have to listen to eleven year olds screach at you to sign their ball, and aren't you a bum if you don't? And, while you're at it, could you sign these dozen baseball cards, too?

The view from the press boxes in major league baseball ranges from mediocre to very good. The best views were in Comiskey Park, the Metrodome and Camden Yards, all of which required rapt attention, otherwise a ball might hit you. One night, Cal Ripken hit a ball to me. The rule in Camden Yards, I quickly found out, was that I had to throw it back in the stands. The last row of seats in the first deck is right in front of the press box, ideal for pre-game visitors who want to drop by, but not great for the great unwashed, who after a few beers, will turn around and ask you what you're doing, and otherwise annoy you. It's a bit like being in a petting zoo. I couldn't imagine a ballpark in New York allowing seats that close to a press box, but overall, it was great being close to the action.

The new press box at Camden Yards was huge. It could hold perhaps 150, but it wasn't intimate. At Memorial Stadium, it was easy to yell over to your colleagues, but here, you had to walk perhaps a hundred feet. It was great having food and drink at your disposal, the bathroom a short walk away, and the sportsticker for updated scores, nearby.

The best seats in the press box belonged to Rex Barney, the long-time public address announcer for the Orioles, Rick Vaughn, and Bob Miller, the public relations officers for the team, and the official scorer. The Baltimore Sun had seats nearby.

The Sun was the only paper in Baltimore. For generations, it had two seperate papers, The Sun and The Evening Sun, which competed vigorously. Late in 1991, the owners, The Times-Mirror Company, which had bought the paper in the mid-eighties, decided to continue publishing seperate papers, but combine the staff. Peter Schmuck, who wrote for the morning entry, and Jim Henneman, who wrote for the evening paper, would now in Schmuck's words, "be buddies instead of competitors." Like many large cities, Baltimore had lost an afternoon paper in the eighties. In 1986, the Hearst's money losing afternoon broadsheet, The News American expired, and their baseball writer, Bill Stetka, became the official scorer.

Peter Schmuck grew up in Orange County, California, wanting to be an archaeologist. Today, he digs up interesting baseball stories for The Sun. While majoring in "conservative arts" at Cal. State-Fullerton, he decided he needed an extra-curricular activity, he joined the campus newspaper reviewing movies, and eventually after contemplating life as a lawyer, he decided to go to journalism school. "As a lawyer, you have to be totally unscrupulous, which is something I'm good at. You also have to take a test, which is something I'm not good at."

He also took a stab at selling cars, but after not selling any, covering high school sports for The Orange County Register seemed more appealing.

He began covering baseball in 1979. "Everybody who they put on baseball got divorced or burned out." He hasn't yet burned out or divorced.

A fan as a child, he learned quickly he was no athlete.

134

"Everybody has a story about their high school coaches not being good judges of talent. My coaches were fine judges of talent. I had none."

He dreamed not of being a sportswriter. "I didn't realize such a profession existed." He's covered the Dodgers, Angels and Orioles, and Rod Carew's 3,000th hit, Reggie Jackson's 500th home run and Don Sutton's 300th victory. He's proud of being there for those players' achievements because on his first road trip with the Dodgers in St. Louis, he decided to take a night off.

The Dodgers had arrived a night early in St. Louis, and Lou Brock had 2,998 career hits. No way Brock would get two hits tonight, Schmuck thought. He was nearly fired when Brock made those two hits.

He attends most of the Orioles' home games, and makes all road trips with the team, though rarely travels with them. The team plane leaves too quickly after games on "getaway day" for him to complete his story, and besides, he wouldn't receive any frequent flyer mileage for flying a charter.

He still enjoys the games, but like most fathers who travel a great deal, pines for his young children. Often, he's not finished working after a night game until 2 A.M., and sometimes he has to arise at 6:30 to meet the team wherever they're playing.

Once, during the 1991 season, Schmuck flew to Seattle early on a Monday morning to catch up with team. He'll arrive at the park perhaps four hours before game time to gather notes for accompanying stories, and write a full 20 inches of copy on the game. He'll try to "squeeze in dinner," write the game story while it's still being played, and compose different stories for each of three editions. He writes from back to front as he's not sure of what his story line will be until the game ends, and if the game is finished early enough he'll try and get some post-game quotes.

After a routine game the previous night at the Kingdome, Schumck learned early the next morning that the team had sent three pitchers to the minor leagues. His plans of sleeping in were shot, and he spent much of the day at the Seattle-Tacoma International

Airport, attempting to find the players who were flying back to Baltimore for his story. He did, but it turned into a second consecutive twenty hour day.

Even on an off-day, a story must be written, and late in the week, a Sunday baseball column must be penned. Schmuck and Henneman now write the column on alternate weeks. Of his life, he says he's paid well, he travels well, but it's still grind. "It's not bad, but there's more to it than most people think."

Schmuck, in his late thirties, has covered some excellent teams, and some poor ones, too. "Bad teams are easier to write about. They have things happen. Interesting things happen to bad teams." Good teams don't necessarily have anything interesting happening.

Jim Henneman is more the old-style baseball writer. Extremely knowledgable, he looks the part. He's in his mid-fifties, a heavy smoker, who has worked for the Orioles as a bat boy, clubhouse attendant and scout, as well as covering the team for several decades.

Henneman is still enamored of the game, and though not an effusive man, he'll gladly impart his knowledge of baseball and writing to an outsider. He seemingly knows everyone in the game, umpires, groundskeepers, scouts, as well as players, managers and coaches. Baltimore baseball fans are well served by this duo.

When a columnist, or an extra writer for The Sun comes to the ballpark, they'll sit near Schmuck or Henneman.

The trio that "runs" the press box, is Vaughn, the public relations officer, Barney, the public address announcer, and Stetka, the official scorer.

Vaughn, and his assistant, Bob Miller, carefully watch the game, announce injury reports or roster moves on the press box public address system, and answer any inquiry from the press. On a home run, they'd intone, "number twelve on a 2-2 pitch," a report that is uniform around major league baseball.

A team's public relations official is not like a p.r. person that I was necessarily used to in my line of work. They actually

136

enjoyed their job, and knew quite a lot about their subject. Their pay was reportedly low, a fraction of what the head of "corporate communications" at a large company might earn.

Vaughn admits that his job should be "Director of Publicity, You're trying to create positive images or spins." For 1991, the team's last year at Memorial Stadium, the theme was nostalgia, for 1992, it was the wonderful new Camden Yards, and for 1993, it was the All-Star Game.

Like Schmuck, he would work ridiculously long hours with little sleep. On home stands, he would arrive at ten for night games, and not leave until after midnight. During the off-season, his work would be cut back to perhaps fifty hours a week. He and his assistant, Bob Miller, would alternate road trips, but once spring training began, he'd often not get a day off for ten weeks.

The interaction between the p.r. department and the writers in most cities is friendly, if not cozy. Having spent many years dealing with corporate p.r. types, I found baseball people more open in providing information, even the negative kind than their corporate bretheren. It is common to find news releases from teams printed verbatim in some large city newspapers, where in a newspaper's business section, an editor would be fired if they printed a company's press release verbatim.

Few baseball reporters or broadcasters could perform their jobs well if it weren't for the reams of information provided to them each day by willing public relations hands. It's also safe to say that baseball teams couldn't survive without the massive free publicity that newspapers, radio and television provide for them.

Bill Stetka spends most of his working hours at Towson State University's alumni office. Like most sane adults, he'd rather be at the ballpark. For all games but Sundays, he is. He earns $75 as the official scorer for Orioles home games. An employee of the American League, he's the guy who keeps questionable no-hitters alive, and won't award Cal Ripken an error.

Say those things, even kiddingly, and he bristles. Arriving about forty-five minutes before game time, he stays about thirty minutes afterward. "When I was covering games" as a beat writer for The News American, "I used to complain about the scoring. I used to see some really atrocious calls, calls that were obviously for the benefit of the home team. Someboday was afraid to call an error because they felt like they have to work here every day."

In 1990, when Ripken was in the midst of a long errorless streak, Stetka removed an error from him, assigning it to Mike Devereaux, a day after the play occurred. As a result of that change, Ripken was able to set a record for most consecutive games at shortstop with an error. Stetka was subject to much abuse because of that call. "Eighty-one games are played on the road. He didn't make errors, there, either."

On the play in question, Stetka had heard after the game that the Cleveland Indians felt the wrong call had been made. He watched the replay once again, as he does before rendering his judgment on many calls, and spoke with all the players involved, as well as umpires and coaches. "It looked like a homer call," he admits, and "it brought a lot of questions about scoring."

Despite the abuse, he jokes that he receives a dollar for the scoring, and seventy-four for the grief, he loves his part-time job. He'd be at the park many nights anyway, and why not get paid for it, and get to eat and park for free as well?

Rex Barney, the public address announcer, has been known to quietly assist Stetka on his calls. Barney tossed a no-hitter for the Brooklyn Dodgers in the forties, and after his career as a fireballing pitcher had been cut short by injury, he decided to try and remain close to the game by being a broadcaster.

After a difficult start in his second career, he came to Baltimore in the sixties, and not long afterward, became the Orioles public adress announcer. Bob Shepard at Yankee Stadium is well known, and lots of fans know who Sherm Feller is. He's behind the mike at Fenway Park, and wrote the lyrics to the popular song of several decades ago, "Summertime."

Before the 1993 season, the San Francisco Giants hired Sherry Davis as the first woman to regularly serve as a baseball team's public address announcer. Few fans could name the public address announcer at their favorite ballpark, but only in Baltimore could Rex Barney become a fan favorite.

He's had a number of health problems since the early eighties, most recently in 1992, he had to have a leg amputated, but through it all, Barney endures. His "Thank youuuuuu" is legendary, and it's common for Baltimore storekeepers to thank their customers in that fashion. "Give that fan a contract" is another favorite; when a fan makes a nice play on a foul ball in the stands, he awards an honorary contract, which is handed to the fan by a nearby usher. If an athletic looking fan boots an easy play, he'll intone: "Give that fan (pause) an error!" His calls are cheered by appreciative Baltimoreans, and while I think he's no Bob Shepard, I have to admit the ballpark and press box just aren't the same when Rex isn't around.

After watching games for years in the stands, and now watching from both there and in the press box, I must admit I prefer the press box. The vantage point is fine, though not as good as my seats eight rows behind the dugout. There aren't any drunks there, there are always knowledgable discussions about baseball, and the bathroom is clean and convenient. The cheeseburgers and crab cakes aren't bad, either. I'm getting itchy for the start of the season. Will it get here already?

Chapter 15:

Playoffs and World Series:

It's Just A Game

I love baseball, but I don't hate football. I simply prefer baseball. The World Series is a far superior athletic event to the Super Bowl, but nearly twice as many people watch a Super Bowl as view a seventh game of the World Series.

The football folks are light years ahead of their baseball bretheren when it comes to marketing, and it shows come Super Bowl time. After the post holiday blues set in, the NFL playoffs begin, and though an occasional undeserving team sneaks in, they're often compelling games. Besides, much is added to a game's excitement when you realize that the loser's season is over, and many of those players won't play for that team again.

Several weeks later, two teams are left, and most years, after an extra week to hype the game, the contest is played. In much of the country, it's cold, and people are more likely to watch television when it's dark outside, and spring is still six weeks away.

Games are better when played on someone's home field. In football, the conference championships are played at the stadium of the team with the best record. The Super Bowl is played on a neutral site, decided upon years in advance. The site of the World Series isn't known for certain until several days before the first game. It wouldn't necessarily be a bad thing if the team with the best record had the extra home game in the League Championship Series and World Series as a reward for excellence during the championship season. Currently, the advantage alternates.

There's not the hype, the office pools, the parties, or the 150 minute pre-game show. I was going to say there wasn't the $175 ticket price, but if you a strip of World Series tickets, it will probably cost you more.

I've been to six World Series, three American League Championship Series, three National League Championship Series, an

All Star Game, and two Super Bowls. The Super Bowl is closer to the All Star Game than to the World Series in many ways. The site of the All Star Game is known several years in advance, and there's a carnival atmosphere surrounding it, too. Both sports have huge exhibits to create interest. But, the All Star Game is an exhibition. There aren't any stock market pundits who claim that the market will react to the winner of the All Star Game. When a team from the old National Football League wins the Super Bowl, the stock market will rise over the balance of the year the large majority of the time. If a team from the old American Football League wins, the market will fall. This theory has been proven correct 23 of the past 26 Super Bowls, and the day after a NFC team wins, the market will usually rise, and this dumb theory is credited.

The World Series is more closely akin to a regular season baseball game than the Super Bowl is to a regular season football game. Many deserving fans do get shut out of the opportunity to see their team play in the World Series, but many more true fans do see the Fall Classic than ever view a Super Bowl.

If you're fortunate enough to see a Super Bowl, you'll hardly see any football fans at all. Perhaps half the tickets are allotted to the participating teams, but even those fans are usually the well heeled ones, the people who can afford cross country trips with little notice. At a Super Bowl, you'll rarely see a guy with a pot belly, a hip flask and a ruddy nose. You'll see men lots of men who resemble Leslie Neilsen and wear Ralph Lauren outfits, and their wives with their designer handbags, neatly combed blonde hair, dazzling smiles and tasteful jewelry. This is true, especially at Super Bowls played in California. Most likely, this is the only football game they've attended since high school. There are few children in attendance; many more get to view World Series games, but there too, it's generally an adult experience.

The accompanying "NFL Experience," theme park, which temporarily occupies many acres adjacent to the Super Bowl sight, is the NFL's paean to its younger fans. With its tests of skill and autograph booths, the league, like the tobacco industry, realizes it must hook future fans in adolesence, if not before.

When baseball expanded its championship series from the best of five games to seven in 1985, I was opposed. I wanted the World Series to stand alone. I was afraid there would be too much of a good thing. In some ways, I was right. The expanded playoffs have been more compelling, often to the detriment of the first games of the World Series. There's that inevitable letdown they talk about after an exciting playoff series. But, there's not two weeks of hype in the papers.

After the hype, how could the game fail to disappoint? With baseball, as a series continues, and a story unfolds, only then does the real hype begin. The seventh game of the World Series is special because there isn't one every year, and there have been many more blowouts in the Super Bowl than there have been four game sweeps in the World Series. (Since the Super Bowl began in 1967, 11 of the 27 games have been decided by three touchdowns or more, while just 3 World Series have taken four games.)

As a fan at the Super Bowl, you're expected to participate in the show by holding up a card or two at halftime, while at a World Series game in the Northeast or Midwest, you stand a fair chance of frostbite in late October. But then again, after the departure of Bowie Kuhn as commissioner, the weather did seem to improve come October. The football people are also smart enough to realize that while few childen attend the game, the future attendees should be able to stay awake throughout, and be able to coherently discuss it with their classmates at school the next day. The baseball people figure that by starting all their World Series games around 8:30, they're maximizing the viewing audience. They're losing youngsters in the East and Midwest whose parents send them to bed at a reasonable hour, or who fall asleep out of habit.

We don't have to go back to the days when many were in work or school for the weekday Series games, and a persnickety boss or teacher prevented you from listening. Sure, there were always a couple of kids with transistor radios, remember them? These future

143

software systems analysts would put a radio under their desk, insert an earplug and listen to the broadcast instead of Social Studies. As a result, productivity in work and school dropped that week, and a lot fewer people saw Sandy Amoros or Willie Mays catch that ball live on television than you think. Don Larsen's perfect game took place in broad daylight, though many more saw Carlton Fisk wave that bad fair.

How about beginning weekday games at about six o'clock? Many are home from work by then in the Eastern half of the country, and they can view the games in their entirety without disturbing sleep. Schoolchildren can complete their homework, and watch a whole game, and those in the Western half of the country will be able to see much more of the game than they would if they were played during daylight hours.

I saw my first League Championship Series in 1973, when the Reds played the Mets, and Pete Rose fought with Bud Harrelson. I simply walked up to the ticket window, and bought the tickets. In 1976, I watched Chris Chambliss hit a home run leading off the bottom of the ninth inning to lead the Yankees over the Royals. You may remember that seemingly much of the crowd ran on the field as soon as Chambliss' ball cleared the wall, and he wasn't able to complete his victory lap. Not long before, George Brett had tied the game with a three run homer. Sitting far up in the right field stands, I knew that Brett's ball was gone by hearing the Royals' bench cheering from several hundred feet away in an otherwise silent Yankee Stadium. In the row in back of me, a few minutes before Chambliss' blast, a fellow had passed out from too much to drink on a chilly evening. I wonder if he has told people that he was there the night that Chambliss hit the home run. If he doesn't begin by saying, "I saw Chambliss hit that home run," he's not lying.

I saw Reggie Jackson hit his three home runs, and Graig Nettles play a marvelous third base one night against the Dodgers. By the time I made it to the 1991 LCS and World Series, I was hardly a post-season virgin.

144

It's a lot different on the field, in the stands, and in the press box for the post-season. The atmosphere is more intense and more exciting. Much more is at stake, and often the tension _is_ in the air. I remember attending my first heavyweight championship bout, in 1977, when Muhammad Ali scored a unanimous decision over Earnie Shavers, in a most entertaining bout. I still recall the excitement that preceeded the beginning of the fight. When the bell sounded for the first round, the crowd was silent, and the tension was palpable.

I haven't been to a boxing match in years, but I wished I had been in the crowd in February 1993, when Riddick Bowe defended his heavyweight championship for the first time. Not for the fight; he easily beat an incompetent Michael Dokes, but for the announcement of the death of tennis great Arthur Ashe. A moment of silence was counted by the bell sounding ten times. I attended the first Yankees game after the death of Thurman Munson in 1979, and found the atmosphere much different. The late Cardinal Terence Cooke remembered Munson, and when his image was shown on the scoreboard, instead of properly showing their respects by silence, the crowd applauded for ten minutes. When the Yankees took the field that night, there was no catcher with them. He followed after the ceremony. That was a spooky baseball atmosphere.

No one is allowed in the clubhouse before a game, and hundreds of media members chase after the key participants on the field. It's often difficult for writers who have covered participating teams daily since spring training to get a private word from a player or manager that they've dealt with regularly and easily. The playoffs and World Series are not just a local story, they're a North American story, and increasingly, a world story. The British, the French, the Japanese, the Latin American countries all have media contingents.

Many writers who aren't on the baseball beat see their only games in October, just as many Americans watch their only baseball on television then. Elaborate pre-game meals are replaced by box lunches, and if you don't like the food, you'll have to fight the long lines at the concession stands with Joe fan.

Only the beat writers who cover major league baseball teams are seated in the main press box. The top columnists, and writers for influential and widely read periodicals are given the best seats in auxiliary press boxes, which are usually seats in the stands converted to use for the media. The participating clubs aren't terribly fond of this arrangement since several hundred seats at the time of peak demand can't be sold.

Some of the seats are not in choice locations, high behind home plate, or deep in the outfield. It was always surprising to see well-known writers craft lovely prose about a game taking place five hundred feet away, and seemingly loving it. At their home ballpark, they'd usually have the best seat in the press box.

After the game, the managers of both teams, and key participants of the winning team would be brought into a mass news conference. Members of the press who were given badges allowing them clubhouse access could further question those players, and attempt to query anyone else.

With so many writers around, it's no wonder that at a World Series, or any other popular championship sporting event, that there is a paucity of original stories.

If you look in unusual places, there are some different stories at each World Series. Take ten year old Thomas Tidwell of Raleigh, North Carolina. He was seated next to me on my flight to Minneapolis for the sixth game of the Series. Wearing a white "Make a Wish Foundation" sweatshirt, I discovered that Thomas had adrenal cancer, and that the commissioner's office had offered him a trip to the World Series. American Airlines had pitched in with round-trip airfare, and shortly after I boarded, Thomas and his father were upgraded to first class.

I wanted to talk to Thomas about his trip, and I followed him up to first class, but the flight attendant said I couldn't stay, even for a minute, but Thomas' dad promised that once aloft, he could come back to talk with me.

A few minutes later, he happily trotted back to my seat,

smiled, and asked, "Do you need any more information?" I was curious about his illness. In all my years of interviewing people, I hadn't yet asked a ten year old about his own mortality. "It was kind of scary, knowing that you could die any day," but today, he confessed, he was just excited thinking about the game. "I get pains in my stomach a lot. I get tired a lot," he admitted. We talked for a bit about baseball, and just then, a passenger in the row in back of us introduced himself. He was Braves' catcher Greg Olson's brother-in-law, and handed Thomas an autographed photo of Olson, and promised to send him Braves memorabilia.

Thomas returned to his seat, and Olson's brother-in-law retrieved a baseball from his case, a ball autographed by all the Braves. I walked up to his seat, handed it to him, and then violated a rule of journalism. I reached into my wallet, gave Thomas ten dollars, and told him to buy something to eat at the game. Sometimes ethics go out the window, especially when a ten-year old cancer patient makes you cry.

The weekend before, the medical story had been Steve Palermo. Arguably the top umpire in the American League, Palermo had been shot in the back several months before while coming to the aid of a robbery victim in Dallas. He had undergone extensive physical therapy, which continues to this day, and had made excellent progress.

He had been invited to throw out the first ball at the initial game of the World Series, and stayed around to watch the second game, before returning home for his therapy. He talked before the game about his fight. Though it was highly unlikely he'd umpire again, he desperately wanted to.

In his braces, he talked about his rehabilitation, and the ovation he had received from the Series crowd. "It reminded me of what I'm missing. Real men do cry," he said, as tears began to stream down his face. "My doctor told me, 'don't be afraid to cry. Rehabilitative patients do cry."

In his rehabilitative hospital were two youngsters, and they would sneak down to Palermo's room to watch baseball on television

147

with him. "We're going to watch Noo-oooo-lan" tonight," one would say, Palermo imitating the child's Texas drawl. "They'd come bogarting into my room bring cookies and ice cream. Then, they'd leave, and my bed would be swimming in cookies and cream," he smiled.

He couldn't wait to be heckled. "You stunk before. You still stink," he could hear the fans say. "Welcome back, Stevie."

"I don't look forward to taking anybody out of a game, but I would enjoy that first one," he predicted. Umpires are never cheered, most fans couldn't name more than a handful. They don't even know how to heckle one. "Come on, blue," is the most common and feeble rejoinder. Because they're on the road so much of the time, they become uniquely close. Palermo had talked for some time, but he had a visit he wanted to make. "I'm going to the umpires room, guys," he said with a smile and a wink as he ambled into his golf cart. "I'll see you later."

If you attend a World Series that the Braves participate in, you'll find that the political correctness movement has spread to baseball. The American Indian Movement dispatches demonstrators to ballparks to protest the Braves, and other sports teams using Native Americans as mascots. "Stop the Chop," one sign read. "Shame on Jane Fonda," read another. "Miami Jews, San Diego Caucasians, New York Negroes," read a third, attempting to draw an analogy between unthinking use of Indian names and the unthinkable use of other ethnic stereotypes.

They've yet to be successful in convincing the Braves, the Cleveland Indians, the Kansas City Chiefs or the Washington Redskins to change their names.

Watching an athlete deal with professional failure is a fascinating part of any sportswriter's job. Charlie Leibrandt was a member of the 1985 World Champion Kansas City Royals, but his 1991 and 1992 Braves lost taut Series.

In 1991, as a starter, he lost the opening game. It wasn't until the sixth game that he pitched again. His first batter, Kirby Puckett, led off the bottom of the eleventh with a home run to tie

148

the World Series at three games each.

After the game, many waited in the Braves locker room for him. He wasn't used to relieving, and not used to pitching on six days rest. Normally ebullient, he was unnerved, it was revealed months later, by the imminent death of his mother-in-law. The horde waited to hear what Leibrandt's thoughts on his baseball misfortune. Two dozen waited for him to shower, two dozen watched him walk slowly and solemnly the fifteen feet from shower to locker. Like gawkers at a tragic accident, we couldn't take our eyes off him. At the back of the throng, I perched on a folding chair to watch this affable man face his inquisitors. This night, he'd make them wait. He slowly pulled on each article of clothing. Two dozen pairs of eyes watched this uncomfortable man dress with his back to them. None attempted to interrupt him. None wanted to be first, but all wanted to hear his explanation.

Finally, he rose, with his tie askew, and turned to walk back to the shower room to dry his curly, thinning hair. Nearly inaudible, he muttered, "Nothing tonight, guys."

In the locker room, Tom Kelly sat and talked about the Series. He played several dozen games as an outfielder for the Twins in 1975, but won two World Series in his first five years as manager. With media training, he had changed from a brusque man to one who could be a fine interview, and easily display humor and candor.

Earlier in the game, his catcher, Junior Ortiz had been called out on strikes without swinging. "That's not good. You're talking about the World Series, and you don't get a swing in the World Series. How can you not get a swing in the World Series? You're going to go down looking in the World Series? That's wrong. If I'm getting a chance to get up to bat in the World Series, I ain't going down looking. I'm getting a chance to swing." Ortiz never played another game for the Twins.

At the end of a press conference, he was leaving when a reporter pleaded for one more question. Kelly stopped, and implored the press to wait. "This may be important. This may be headline stuff."

"You've seen a lot of baseball in your day. One word answer, is this a classic Series up till now?"

"Never mind, keep going," Kelly guffawed to the exiting press. "They tell me it's very good. They tell me it's great."

The next night, in the last game of one of the classic World Series in history, Kelly struggled. After Jack Morris had completed his ninth scoreless inning, he wanted to take him out. Bring in Rick Aguilera to begin the tenth inning of this 0-0 tie, he thought, he'd be fresh. He told Morris he appreciated what he had done for the club.

Morris was having none of it. He wanted to continue. "T.K., I'm fine, I'm fine, save Aggie," he pleaded. Morris implored Kelly to ask pitching coach Dick Such his opinion. Such thought Morris could continue. Kelly relented, and decided to leave him in. "I said, what the hell, it's just a game."

Chapter 16:

I Wouldn't Let Baseball Die

Like many other passionate baseball fans, I always thought an ideal job would be commissioner of baseball. Get to go to any game you want, wherever you want, with the best seats. If I were commissioner, I could do wonderful things to improve the game I love, you probably think. Wake up, pal, if Peter Ueberroth and Fay Vincent couldn't resolve the designated hitter dichotomy, how could you, much less, restore labor peace to the sport.

If I were commissioner, I would immerse myself in the job, leaving little time to deal with owners. Poor Fay Vincent, if only he wouldn't have had to deal with the people who employ him. Then, he could actually have improved the sport.

In travelling around baseball in recent years, I've had the opportunity to see the game behind the scenes as well as in the stands, and while not naive before undertaking this self-assigned task, I've developed a greater awareness of the business side of the game. Ray Miller, the astute pitching coach of the Pittsburgh Pirates, jokingly told me that he would impose a $10,000 fine on any man in uniform who discussed money once spring training began. I wouldn't go that far because many fans have become surprisingly astute about the games' economics in recent years. Some are small business owners, some work for large corporations, and some are doctors and lawyers. They face economic decisions each day in their own professional lives, and while they seek to escape at the ballpark, they're able to bring their own experience to participate in informal informed discussions on the business of the sport.

Money isn't going away, and neither is artificial turf, domes, nor the designated hitter. But, there are some things that the commissioner could change.

As I write this, baseball has been without a commissioner for half a year, and the lack of leadership has been apparent to all, save for the owners. Along with several million other allegedly sane adults, I've had a secret dream to be the baseball commissioner. The main drawback is that you work for the owners. As much as I might like to, I wouldn't be able to ignore them. If you do, you're no longer allowed to sit in front of everyone else.

There have been a few positive developments in baseball recently. Minority employment is up, and the Cincinnati Reds have discarded the polyester pullover uniforms I despise in favor of the old-style button down tops. The Pittsburgh Pirates decided to close off some 12,000 seats at Three Rivers Stadium, attempting to give the park more of a feeling of intimacy, and also to create a rush to buy tickets in advance.

For the first time in memory, a city, the one in which I live, Baltimore, will host major and minor league baseball simultaneously. For several years, I mourned the passing of Memorial Stadium, thinking the Orioles didn't need a new home, and thought I'd weep when the last game was played there.

Cal Ripken hit into a double play, and after the completion of his victory, Detroit pitcher Frank Tanana saluted the stadium. An evocative program recalling the greats, near-greats, mediocrities and bit players of Oriole history followed, leaving all who attended grateful for having come.

There would never be baseball there again, though barely a month later, I attended my first college football game. The University of Maryland hosted Penn State at Memorial Stadium, and the Nittany Lions won easily. It was cold and windy, and I, a former season ticket holder of the woeful Colts, had forgotten what an awful place it was to watch football.

Upon leaving that freezing November day, I assumed that I was to return only if the NFL deigned to grant Baltimore an expansion franchise.

Little did I know that the Hagerstown Suns, a AA affiliate of the Orioles would be moving to Bowie, about 30 miles south of Baltimore, near Annapolis, for the 1993 season. The Suns had been forced to leave Hagerstown, a city some 75 miles west of Baltimore, because their park no longer met the requirements major league baseball set for AA franchises. Hagerstown would host a A affiliate of the Toronto Blue Jays while the owners of the Suns relocated their team to a new park in Prince Georges County.

As the 1993 season approached, construction on the home of the Bowie BaySox had yet to begin. Where would they play? Some suggested they temporarily move to Frederick, about forty miles west of Baltimore, where the Keys, an Oriole A franchise play. The owners of the BaySox and the Keys are one and the same, and the Keys, in a lovely new park, had managed to outdraw many AA and AAA franchises. Others suggested Washington's RFK Stadium or Shipley Field, at the University of Maryland. The Orioles suggested Memorial Stadium, and though some of the time the Orioles and the BaySox would be playing at home simultaneously, the deal was agreed upon in early February.

Having attended just one complete minor league game, in Harrisburg, Pennsylvania, and four innings of another, played at the conclusion of an Oriole game in Memorial Stadium, I hardly qualify as a devotee of the bushes. Much to my surprise, when plans were announced for the BaySox' temporary home, I was overjoyed. Perhaps I'd attend only a handful of games, and perhaps the crowds in the 50,000 seat stadium would be embarrasssingly small. Still, it was lovely to contemplate the thought of baseball nearly every day during the summer.

I never knew I'd want access to minor league baseball, too, but I decided upon my appointment as commissioner, I would require all fans to spend some time in the minors. I learned baseball as a fan on the major league level, unlike almost all players. Though Jim Abbott, Pete Incaviglia and Dave Winfield have never played minor league ball, it's healthy for the rest of us fans to watch the skills develop in some, and be obvious that those skills aren't present in most.

My biggest complaint about baseball is that the rabid fan is taken for granted. When I was a child, one of my dreams was to have season tickets to the games. Since 1982, I've held a 25% interest in a Baltimore Oriole season ticket, truly a wise investment. The seats are eight rows behind the Oriole dugout, about 15 feet from home plate. I'm hardly alone in owning season tickets. A generation ago, it was a rare and well-to-do fan that held season tickets, and a club was lucky to sell several thousand seats a year. Today, the Orioles sell nearly 30,000 seats for the entire season, and many clubs have plans for fans who can attend perhaps a third of the games, or just night games, or just Sunday games.

While the clubs have done a great job at convincing fans of the necessity of buying seats ahead of time, once the tickets are sold, the fans are forgotten about. The clubs don't know who uses the seats. My season tickets are in a friend's name, and the Orioles have no way of knowing if I ever pay to get into games.

In the early eighties, as the airline industry felt the effects of deregulation, and fare wars became common, new ways of marketing were unveiled. While occasional pleasure travellers could be rewarded with low fares because they had the flexibility to plan their trips far in advance, the business traveller felt ignored. The business traveller made the airlines, and while the airlines couldn't lower their fares for customers who bought their ticket just a few days or even a few hours before their trip began, they could reward them.

They did, with the frequent traveller program, and while the travel weary flyer may not want to take yet another journey, it's a way of saying "thank you" to a valued customer.

Baseball thanks its fans poorly. The giveaways are rarely useful, usually items such as cheap tote bags suitable for toting only to games.

Why not institute a frequent fan program? Reward fans for dollars spent on tickets, food and souvenirs. If they spend thousands of dollars, send fans on a road trip with the club, or let them have a skybox for a night. Let the loyal bleacher fan who can't afford to lay out money for a box seat for an entire season sit in a great seat occasionally.

How about starting a room for fans to wait out rain delays? For $125 a year, airline travellers get to hang out at clubs before

154

their flights. Why not have rooms with televisions, couches, food and drink, restrooms and reading material to entertain those who would pay to avoid the crowds under the stands during delays? They could be used between games of the odd doubleheader or if a fan arrives early on an oppressively humid day.

One of the joys of sitting in the press box is being on the inside. If a player is scratched from the starting line-up unexpectedly, the fans don't know the reason why. The press does, and while it's announced on radio and television, often the fan doesn't know the reason why a regular player isn't playing. They'll have to wait to read about it in the next day's newspaper. Why not have clubs summarize the day's news on the message board just prior to the start of the game? Tell fans why someone isn't playing, who had to leave the club because of the impending birth of a child or a death in the family.

Explain scoring decisions promptly and completely; the Pirates are good at this, and if there's a controversial play, summarize and explain it. I sat high up in left field for the 1978 World Series, and during the fourth game, I never knew the argument on the field was about Reggie Jackson's attempt, or lack of one, to elude a thrown ball. It was a turning point in the game, and possibly the series, and it would have helped to summarize these unusual plays for those who actually care about the nuances of the game.

Media guides are quite useful for writers and broadcasters. They're now on public sale. Daily press notes, compiled by the club's public relations department are invaluable for writers and broadcasters, too. Why not print up 500 or 1000 of both team's notes and statistics and sell them to the hard core? The clubs would be doing a service for the cognoscenti, and making some money, too.

The clubs do a great job at the casual fan, and the younger fan. Recorded music has replaced organs at most parks. I would prefer a combination of the two, myself, but most of the younger fans like the music at the games. Save for the Phillie Phanatic,

I'm not a mascot fan, but for children, I suppose they do have a place. Giveaways of balls, bats and gloves for kids aren't a bad idea, and it's no coincidence that when interest in baseball was waning in the mid to late sixties, teams began giving away items, and attendance began to rise. Today, the children who attended the first bat and cap days are taking their own youngsters to the games.

Instead of giving every fan who attends a certain game the same item, whether they visit the park regularly or not, I would reward perhaps one in twenty fans at designated games with truly valuable prizes. Give them a team warm-up jacket, or good seats to a game, give them a reason to come. On some Fan Appreciation Days, trips and season tickets are awarded, but they're only awarded to a handful of fans, and they're never in your section. Make sure on this giveaway day, that a fan in every section is rewarded.

The food at some parks has improved in recent years, all the way to edible. In fact, the crab cakes at Camden Yards aren't half bad. Some parks, notably Tiger Stadium and Fenway Park feature poor ballpark fare. Require each franchise to stock at least one item at the concession stands indigenous to the area. In Philadelphia, you can get cheesesteaks, in MIlwaukee, bratwurst, but guys, show some imagination in Detroit or Boston.

As a youngster, I learned almost from the time I could walk that when the National Anthem was played, I was to remove my baseball cap. I rarely wear a cap today, but others do, and next time you go to a game, watch and see how many don't know, or don't care to remove their hats. Perhaps a few of them are bald, and modest, and I did learn this before the Vietnam War made patriotism unfashionable, but clubs, if you insist on playing the National Anthem before each game, please ask the fans to remove their hats.

By the way, I've found nothing in the Constitution that mandates the National Anthem be played before each game. When you were in school, did you know what the words for The Pledge of Allegiance were? Because you had to recite it every day, didn't it lose its meaning? Wouldn't it be better if the National Anthem were performed before selected games, say on Sundays and holidays? What does baseball have to do with patriotism, anyway?

If you insist on playing a patriotic song before a game, why not follow the lead of a few teams and substitute "God Bless America" or "America the Beautiful" for "The Star Spangled Banner." Besides, I have a good singing voice, I'm told, and the Anthem is one hard song to master. But, if you continue to play the Anthem, no more nine year old girls warbling it, please?

I wasn't surprised at the reactions of the players to the press when I got inside baseball. I'd read enough about it to know that they abided and rarely admired each other. The aloofness of a few star players surprised me, but the openness of some managers was a joy.

John Oates was outstanding. He was honest and civil. He didn't butter writers up, and tried to answer questions honestly, and only occasionally snapped at a stupid question. All managers are available to the press immediately after the games. Most players are much harder to find. They'll hang out in the trainer's room or the player's lounge, both off-limits to the press until the writers get tired of waiting. With the length of games, night games, particularly, meeting deadlines can be tough, and writers can't wait for an hour after a three hour thirty minute game for a player to deign to mumble a few cliches to a writer.

It amazed me, to say the least, how grateful writers were for just a few words from a player. Most players are fairly cooperative when cornered, a few are great copy, and a few are openly hostile. Players ought to realize that most writers don't care about their personal problems, and if they'll spend just a few minutes after a game, it will help everybody do their job. Why not require all players, except those who need immediate medical attention, to sit in front of their lockers for ten minutes after the locker rooms are opened. The players will find that most writers aren't out for blood, they just have a job to do, like the players.

As a television producer, I've discovered the joys of media training in recent years. I can often tell when a guest or prospective guest has undergone media training, but the viewer can't. Some professional teams have sent their athletes for training; perhaps all should. While you're at it, please teach athletes not to refer to themselves in the third person. "This wasn't a typical Roger Clemens start" or "When Jose Canseco gets hot, he can carry a ballclub."

The clubs ought to attempt to convince all players how much the media can help a player. I realize that if a guy is earning several million dollars a season, that media exposure isn't likely to help him, but ask Rick Dempsey how much the media helped him? Even though I've never met Pete Rose, he was noted for being quite cooperative, and that may be a reason it took so long to for his gambling problems to come to light.

After I've educated the players, I'll try to educate the fans. One of the most precious moments of the 1986 World Series was when Vin Scully summarized a tiresome ballpark pastime. When Roger Clemens faked a throw to second base, and the crowd jeered, Scully intoned, "As inevitably as night follows day, the cries of 'balk.'"

For years, I've been decrying the uninformed, but Vinnie did it better than anyone. Why can't these fans learn? Why don't they understand when the tarp is being removed and the grounds crew looks for a moment as if they're reapplying it, that they're just dumping water? Why do they have to boo? Why must they boo each intentional walk of a home team player?

How about fan education days? Why not require all players, coaches and managers to appear once before several hundred fans for a question and answer session about the games? Some teams have tried this, and all should. It would also help bridge the perceived distance between fans and players.

Requiring that all players spend forty-five minutes signing autographs on a pre-selected day once a year wouldn't be a bad idea, either. Watching baseball from the inside, I've come to have less sympathy for the players' complaints in dealing with the press, and more for their complaints in dealing with autograph seekers. Earlycomers who want to watch batting practice are often engulfed by the signature seekers, and what the players say is true, if you sign one, you have to sign them all. I wasn't much of an autograph seeker as a kid, but I was disappointed when I cornered Don Drysdale at a park in Brooklyn during a personal appearance, and asked for his autograph, only to be waved away by this giant of a man, who said "no autographs." Don't prohibit autograph seeking, it's hard to change a pastime of millions of American kids, and some adults, but make sure that a fan knows that next Sunday he'll be able to get Kirby Puckett's autograph. It wouldn't hurt if parents would cease giving their youngsters fifteen dollars to get an autograph from a player at a card show who doesn't even acknowledge their presence. If parents stopped supporting this cottage industry, it would dry up, and fast!

Games are too long. Umpires ought to enforce the strike zone as written in the rule book, and force batters to bat. Don't let them step out of the box after every pitch. Make pitchers pitch. Don't allow them to dawdle, and don't let catchers slowly rise after a pitch, and walk the ball a third of the way to the mound before returning it.

Umpires should have the right to call a game, even before it begins. I've seen clubs call games hours before the scheduled starting time when a small crowd was expected, and their pitching staff was battered, only to see the skies brighten forty-five minutes before gametime. Put the responsibility on the umpires at all times, not just during the last series of the year between the clubs. Don't let them wait all night to begin a game. Late season waits of three hours are not uncommon. Allow no game to begin more than two hours after the scheduled start. The fans do have to go to work or school, most of them, anyway, and it's unfair to make them wait until 10 P.M. or later, for a game to begin.

Don't cancel games that have already begun because of rain, suspend them. A game should be nine innings, not seven or six. If four innings have been played, and a batter already has two home runs, those home runs should count in the records, and the game should be resumed at the earliest time possible. Adoption of this rule would prevent delaying tactics by a team that's trailing in the fifth inning when the skies open up. The umpires probably wouldn't wait as long as they do now to call games if they had the option of suspending them.

Treat the umpires better. Pay them well, and combine the umpiring staffs of the two leagues so that they might not have to travel as much. If an umpire lives in the East, and he's an American League arbiter, Baltimore, Boston and New York are the only cities remotely close to home. If the staffs were combined, he could also call Phillie and Met games. With higher pay and improved working conditions, perhaps they wouldn't be so confrontational, and they'd walk away from arguments instead of challenging players and managers.

In other sports, a coach who enters the field of play is penalized. Why should a manager be allowed to enter the field of play to dispute a call? He should be allowed on the field only to change a pitcher or check on an injured player. A player should be allowed to question a call just as in other sports, but imagine being an umpire when Earl Weaver, Billy Martin or Leo Durocher charged onto the field, kicking dirt and loudly cursing. The only reason managers are allowed to run onto the field is because it's always been done that way. While I've enjoyed the antics of the afore-mentioned managers a number of times, it would lessen the perceived threats the umpires face. Don't eliminate a manager questioning a call from the sanctity of the bench, but if he has a message for an ump, he'll send it with a player.

While umpires may not know the rules of scoring, who better to decide what's a hit or an error, a wild pitch or a passed ball than an umpire? Have an official scorer to maintain records, but let the umpire decide on controversial calls. He's not afraid to make a call with the game on the line, why not eliminate "home town" scoring decisions. We've all seen or heard of games where in the late inning of a no-hitter being thrown by a pitcher of the home team, a scorer decides that an apparent error is a hit. Let

160

the ump call it.

And while I'm at it, I think I'll get rid of the designated hitter, artificial turf, and most of the domes, too.

It looks like the snow has melted, and my garden is beginning to come alive. Daylight savings time is here, Opening Day must be tomorrow, and I better get there. See you at the park.

Chapter 17:
Expansion: Early Birds, Snow Birds And Mile High Birds

I must confess. I was so busy last year covering Orioles games for U.P.I., working on a number of free-lance projects, and performing my day job that I never did get to Memorial Stadium to see the Bay Sox play--but my intentions were good.

I did mean to go out to Denver, too, but I didn't want to run into Yogi Berra there. You know, his old joke about not wanting to go to a restaurant: "Nobody goes there anymore, it's too crowded."

Mile High Stadium, where the Colorado Rockies played in 1993, and will play in 1994, drew crowds that boggled the mind that first year. Never did the Rockies attract as few as 40,000 fans, and for the season, totaled nearly 4.5 million.

As the season neared its end, I decided to follow the pennant race and see the Orioles in Milwaukee and Cleveland instead of visiting Denver. Unfortunately, the Orioles came apart on that trip, but I did get to witness one of the final baseball games to be played in Cleveland Stadium. I knew I'd have another shot a Mile High, but as I reminded myself, don't blow this one because next year, they'll move a few miles away to **their** version of Camden Yards, Coors Field.

I've been to Denver a few times. I'm not a skiier, and besides they don't ski at Aspen, Vail or Steamboat Springs during most of the baseball season, anyway. I prefer to spend my time at "The Tattered Cover," arguably America's best bookstore. (I hope they carry this book.) If you're ever in Denver, and like bookstores, don't miss this place. It features helpful, knowledgeable salespeople and comfortable easy chairs, too. I don't think you're likely to run into too many ballplayers there. Steve Carlton, who lives some hours away in Durango, Colorado, was a regular at "The Strand Book Store" in New York, but he was sort of different. I'll have to tell you what I thought of Mile High baseball next year.

I did see the Rockies play one of their first games though, in St. Louis, and I was fortunate enough to see the Florida Marlins play a number of times in 1993.

This fearless prognosticator forecast that both the Rockies and Marlins would be among the worst teams ever to play big league baseball. In fact, neither finished in last place, nor lost 100 games. I assumed Florida and Colorado were locks for both "accomplishments." Colorado featured a real live batting champion, Andres Galarraga, and Florida, a number of fine players including Bryan Harvey, Gary Sheffield and Walt Weiss. Weiss left the Marlins at season's end to sign with the Rockies.

For now, the Marlins play in charmless Joe Robbie Stadium, located in the northwest corner of Dade County, far from downtown Miami. There is a neighborhood of sorts just west of the ballpark. (Actually, Joe Robbie looks more like a stadium.) The late Miami Dolphins owner built the stadium with his own money, and immediately began campaigning for a major league baseball team, realizing that a handful of football games weren't going to support his project.

The neighborhood features modest homes with bored looking residents and a few cul-de-sacs that I discovered one night when traffic was rerouted in front of the stadium by police due to a gruesome accident. A few blocks south is a busy commercial area, and there are buses that take fans to the games, but it's so spread out, so soulless, even if there is a neighborhood nearby. I guess it's hard for this northeasterner who has trouble with five digit street addresses in Baltimore County to think there could be a ballpark located on North West 199th Street. Scalpers hold up worn cardboard signs for motorists, asking for or selling tickets while a few feet away, teenagers in small dune buggies perform wheelies in the rough sand that borders the stadium. All the while, traffic is efficiently moved in and out of the park.

The Marlins do a nice job, though, with what they've been given. Owner Wayne Huizenga, he of the Blockbuster Video fortune, has explored the idea of building a park for his Marlins, and not his newly acquired Dolphins, to be part of a sports and entertainment complex, with an indoor arena for hockey and basketball. He also owns the Florida Panthers of the National Hockey League.

Perhaps the Marlins will play in Fort Lauderdale in a few years. In any case, I'm glad I saw them in their first months. I viewed them at their high point of the season, when they swept the three-time defending National League East champion Pittsburgh Pirates in a four game series. They actually closed to within a game of .500 in mid-June before reverting to type.

I was unprepared for the lack of knowledge these fans possessed. After all, many had migrated south from the large metropolitan areas of the Northeast and Middle West. They were supposed to know baseball. They grew up playing it, watching it in person, and since they moved to Florida, presumably have watched a game or two on television. Florida **is** the spring home of most major league teams. They didn't act as if they knew baseball. Callers into those ubiquitous sportstalk shows thought it was possible for the Marlins to challenge for second place, and maybe after the season sign a big name free agent or two to put them "over the top."

These people were obviously not used to watching major league baseball in person. They would shriek at simple foul balls, didn't know how to judge the trajectory of a batted ball, and were unfamiliar with basic rules and strategies. But, as in Colorado, they were easy to please and showed up in hugh numbers. Baseball's two fears about expanding into Denver and Miami were weather related: snowouts in Denver in April and rainouts in Miami in the summer. Neither fear materialized. The Marlins were rained out twice, and it didn't snow in Denver in April.

The baseball moguls didn't worry about dilution of talent, especially pitching. 15-14 World Series games don't bother them, Charlie Hough being the ace of an expansion team staff doesn't bother them, either. This expansion was so successful, why not try again in a couple of years?

With this expansion such a financial success, the owners are supposedly looking to St. Petersburg, and its white elephant, the Suncoast Dome, and to Phoenix, as sites for its next goaround.

The Marlins put a giant grey tarp around the upper deck of Joe Robbie, converting a football stadium that seats over 70,000 to a ballpark seating nearly 30,000 fewer. They don't sell "club" seats in fair territory. Club seats are in the expensive middle deck, where I sat.

The ballpark is an appealing sea of aqua and teal with a large number of this culturally diverse crowd wearing those teal colored caps. It was nice to see such a mix of people, lots of young people seeing baseball for the first time, and lots of older people in mild weather experiencing a hardball rebirth of sorts.

The playing field was asymmetrical, the furthest point being 434 feet in left center, with 330 feet to left and 345 to right. The bullpens were square, away from the field, as they are in Pittsburgh, and the tarp was positioned in front of the right field bullpen.

There were some interesting touches. The teal hand operated scoreboard in left field with inning by inning scores, and line-ups presented that way, too. A huge modern scoreboard was present as well. It made for a nice complement. Inside at concession stands were Cuban foods that I was unfamiliar with, but some of them looked like either Knishes or chicken patties. Presumably to appeal to tobacco loving Cubans, handmade cigars were on sale, too. Fortunately, I didn't see too many of those being sold or smoked.

The stadium is enclosed. If there wasn't an upper deck covered by a grey tarp, you wouldn't see what passes for a vista in northwestern Dade County--parking lots and highways.

It's also air conditioned, or part of it is. I had purchased those club level seats for $30 a ticket. I decided that if I wanted to experience baseball in Florida, I shouldn't sit in the press box. It turned out my seats were excellent ones, behind home plate, just a few feet in front of the enclosed press box.

During the first game I attended, "Billy the Marlin" began dancing between innings to "The Hokey Pokey," and I didn't learn until I was driving back to my hotel that the somewhat shy middle-aged gentleman who had been coaxed out onto the field was none other than the owner of the team, Mr. Huizenga. I'm sure George Steinbrenner wouldn't know how to put his right foot out --especially after being put out of baseball for several seasons.

The fans cheered the owner lustily, as they did most any favorable development. The public address announcer would solemnly intone "top half of inning 3." This could encourage a mild cheer on occasion, too.

I've never been a fan of air conditioning, use it only at home or in my car for the absolutely most oppressive of days, but it was nice to walk in the club level of Joe Robbie Stadium before the game in comfort. It didn't feel like a ballpark, sidling up to the bar to buy a Coke amid the people who had no idea that it was illegal for a fielder to throw his glove at a batted ball, but that was okay. I've come to realize--albeit slowly--that baseball will need its own Fox Network--and it's not likely to be The Baseball Network. You have to appeal to the Club Med, Hard Rock Cafe and Planet Hollywood crowd. I may not watch "Melrose Place" and "Beverly Hills 90210," but your prospective fans do.

The last night I was in Florida, I decided to stop off at a local restaurant and have my pre-game meal. By the way, the cheeseburgers in Joe Robbie Stadium were perfectly acceptable. I ate in a locally renowned joint in Hollywood, but had forgotten that the only people who eat in South Florida before six P.M. were the senior citizens who wished to partake of the so-called "early bird" dinners, featuring reduced portions and reduced prices.

I was the only diner under the age of 80, it seemed. My father, who is in his mid-seventies, likes to joke that when he visits Florida, the residents refer to him as "Kid." As I sat eating my reduced portion at my reduced price, I realized that someday I would be among those elderly diners, and countless personal and professional crises from now, I hoped I would still have a baseball game to look forward to after dinner.

Acknowledgements

I have so many people to thank for this book, and I'm sure I'll forget a few people. First, to my friend Mike Klein, thank you for the idea, and the continual encouragement. For Mike English, thank you for setting up my computers and answering all my technical questions. For John Davis, thank you for being a great boss. For Dottie Burlage, thanks for all the little things that don't show up in the box scores. For Marsha and Buddy Potler, thank you for all the quiet support, and thanks for keeping Susan company. For Bill Gildea, Eliot Cohen and Mike Gesker, I can never repay your friendship and support.

Thanks, too, to Rick Vaughn and Bob Miller of the Baltimore Orioles, Andy Musser, broadcaster of the Philadelphia Phillies, and Jerry Howarth, broadcaster of the Toronto Blue Jays, I couldn't have done it without all of you.

To the Orioles, especially Manager John Oates and former coach, now scout, Curt Motton, thanks for all your time.

To the guys in the press box, especially Peter Schmuck, Mark Maske, Jim Henneman, John Delcos, Dave Ginsberg, Thom Loverro, Joe Gross, Bob Brown, Gordon Beard, David Hill and David Simone, thanks for everything.

There were others whose help shouldn't be forgotten: Ed Novak, Ken Day, Bonitta Best, LethaJoy Martin, and last, but certainly not least, Steve Slezak, whom I promised I wouldn't forget.

And most important, thanks to everyone who kept asking me when the book was coming out. It's out, so you can stop asking.